# Understanding
# the Buddha's Light Philosophy

佛 光 學

© 2002 Buddha's Light Publishing

by Venerable Master Hsing Yun
translated by Fo Guang Shan International Translation Center
edited by Ven. Miao Jie
Cover designed by Mei-Chi Shih


Published by Buddha's Light Publishing
3456 S. Glenmark Drive
Hacienda Heights, CA 91745
U.S.A.
Tel: (626) 923-5143
Fax: (626) 923-5145
e-mail: **itc@blia.org**

ISBN: 0-9715612-2-2
Library of Congress Control Number: 2001099613

# Table of Contents

# Foreword

This modernization of Buddhism is a big job and therefore takes a great deal of effort. This was especially true regarding the need for a complete set of textbooks on Buddhism. In 1957, I was contacted by a Buddhist-sponsored middle school in the Philippines. Through senior monk Yin Hsun, these honorable people asked me to compile a set of Buddhist textbooks for them. I decided, because I felt inadequately prepared for such a large undertaking.

During the 1960s, Singapore promoted the Chinese language and wished to assemble a set of Buddhist textbooks. When Venerable Zhang Jue consulted me about the task, I declined again due to my special circumstances at that time.

The development and extensive practice of Buddhism in Taiwan makes it quite clear that there is an urgent need for a complete set of Buddhist textbooks. The current editions of Buddhist textbooks, including those compiled by Mr. Fang Lun, are for beginning, intermediate, and advanced students. Texts that have been assembled by various Buddhist organizations are not widely valued in Buddhist communities.

In 1990, I made a vow to put together a set of textbooks totaling one hundred thousand words, simply entitled *Buddhism*. After combining the works of eminent Buddhist elders along with the theories of various Buddhist schools, my first compilation amounted to three million words! When first published, this set of textbooks served as lecture reference material for members of Buddha's Light International Association, and for the disciples of Fo Guang Shan. However, it did not circulate in the outside world.

In recent years, the need for Buddhist textbooks has increased. I noted this growing of interest to my disciple, Miao Qing, who then acquired the assistance of many volunteers. All of them, ranging from the staff of Fo Guang Shan to teachers and students from the Buddhist colleges, responded enthusiastically. But the style of a textbook differs from that of a narrative; it takes a professional touch to accomplish the task. We made a suggestion to the Monastery Affairs Committee at Fo Guang Shan to establish a Transcription Office. In addition to writing from dictation and copying manuscripts, we expanded this office's function to undertake the task of compiling the preliminary draft of the *Fo Guang Textbooks*.

At the time, the *Fo Guang Textbooks* were my most important work. When traveling abroad, and even while recuperating from an ailment, I took Transcription Office clerks with me to the Fo Guang Outreach Center on the golden shores of Australia to write. While visiting our branch temple in Hong Kong, I worked with a single-minded commitment on the textbooks. I focused on this task as much as possible, and accomplished my avowed wish after making several trips to America, Europe, and Australia.

In order to make the content of the textbooks more inclusive and judicious, I invited eminent Buddhist elders and scholars to assist me. For example, for the chapter on Tibetan Buddhism, I especially invited Lama Tian Pi-shuang, a member of the Board of Directors of the Chinese and Tibetan Cultural Association, to proofread the manuscript. For the essay entitled "A Summary of Taoism," I requested comments from a seasoned expert on Taoism, Mr. Kung Peng-cheng, president of Nan Hua University. For the article entitled "Religions Among People," I invited an expert in this field, professor Cheng Chih-ming, to evaluate the manuscript. A senior practitioner of Yi Guan Dao, Mr. Lin Yu-te, also participated in this endeavor by reviewing the article entitled "A Summary of Yi Guan Dao." Furthermore, articles on Judaism and Christianity were read and corrected by scholars or teachers of each religion. Monastics of Fo Guang Shan such as Venerables Tzu Hui, Tzu Jung, Tzu Jia, Tzu Yi, and Yi Kung were involved in reviewing manuscripts, checking references, polishing the text, and making corrections. Although the contents of the *Fo Guang Textbooks* were conceived and established by me, their completion depended upon the participation and efforts of the disciples of Fo Guang Shan as well as various others. I thank all of them for their valuable contributions.

We began to assemble the *Fo Guang Textbooks* in 1995. This task took five years, but we finally finished, having completed our job on the eve of the two thousandth anniversary of the spread of Buddhism eastward into China. I am grateful for the help of the Triple Gem, the work that was done by eminent scholars, the assistance provided to me by the Buddhist writings of my predecessors, the active publishing enterprises of Taiwanese Buddhism, and the work of all Buddhist elders. All of these conditions gave birth to the *Fo Guang Textbooks*.

There are four basic characteristics of the *Fo Guang Textbooks*.
First, each set contains twelve volumes:
1. Triple Gem: the Buddha, the Dharma, and the Sangha
2. The Truth of Buddhism
3. Practice and Verification of the Bodhisattva
4. The History of Buddhism
5. A Summary of Buddhist Traditions
6. Practical Buddhism
7. The Common Sense of Buddhism
8. Buddhism and Worldly Knowledge
9. Exploring Issues in Buddhism
10. A Summary of Religion

There are twenty chapters in each volume, and about two thousand words per chapter. Although space restrictions create obstacles for the expounding of the vast and profound Dharma, footnotes are used to clarify each article and to assist students with reference gathering.

Second, the *Fo Guang Textbooks* assist practitioners with both learning basic concepts as well as multi-functional learning. As Buddhism places the Triple Gem at its center, we thus place "Triple Gem: the Buddha, the Dharma, and the Sangha" in the first volume. Once readers have confidence in the Triple Gem, they can swim freely in the sea of the Dharma.

The second volume, "The Truth of Buddhism," and the third volume, "Practice and Verification of the Bodhisattva," are extensions of the Triple Gem. In this sense, the first three volumes offer the structural theory of the Triple Gem. "The History of Buddhism" is related to "A Summary of Buddhist Traditions." "Practical Buddhism," "Common Sense of Buddhism," and "Buddhism and Worldly Knowledge" are also correlated with one another. Finally, "Exploring Issues in Buddhism" and "A Summary of Religion" prompts public understanding of issues within Buddhism.

We placed "Understanding the Buddha's Light Philosophy" in the eleventh volume, because Fo Guang Shan has, for several decades, advocated modernization, becoming focused on the world in which we live, and the systematization of Buddhism. By focusing on Fo Guang Shan and Buddha's Light International Association, various concepts and goals are defined to assist the reader in understanding the direction and the future development of humanistic Buddhism.

To enable beginners to understand the profundity and vastness of the Dharma through the works of our eminent Buddhist predecessors, we selected some historic sutras and excellent essays to complete "Selected Articles of Buddhist Literature." A brief introduction was added to each article to help readers more deeply understand and appreciate the Dharma.

Third, although the number of words limits the content of each chapter of the *"Fo Guang Textbooks"*, teachers and readers can consult the footnotes that are provided. The pictures and exercises that are provided await full utilization by both teachers and readers.

It should be mentioned that the lack of references to original sources in some of the footnotes is a drawback in this set of textbooks. However, Fo Guang Shan reference books such as the "Fo Guang Tripitaka," the "Scripture Treasures of Chinese

Buddhism," and especially the "Fo Guang Buddhist Dictionary" are available for further study. These supplemental texts can clarify the teaching of the *"Fo Guang Textbooks."*

Fourth, the *"Fo Guang Textbooks"* are not aimed at scholars or experts. These volumes are designed to assist the beginner who is in need of an understanding of Buddhism. Stressing a foundation of basic Buddhist knowledge, the content of these textbooks is unsuitable for scholarly research and verification. In the introductions to the various Buddhist traditions, no preference is shown for any school, and all of the teachings of all schools are covered. In exploring the history of Buddhism, the interruptions in the continuity of the spread of Buddhism are acknowledged, for this may serve to assist the future reformation and improvement of Buddhism.

Through this set of textbooks, teachers and readers can attain an overall understanding of Buddhism. In this sense, it is our hope that these twelve volumes will be used in monasteries and Buddhist colleges, and even utilized in seminars or study groups sponsored by Buddhist organizations. We fervently hope that this set of textbooks will serve as a stepping-stone of reference for people taking an interest in studying Buddhism.

By chance, the publication of this set of textbooks coincided with the year 2000, which also happens to be the $2000^{th}$ anniversary of the spreading of Buddhism eastward into China. At the turning of the new millennium, I sincerely wish that all readers of these textbooks would send me their comments and thoughts.

Hsing Yun
Fo Guang Shan
May, 1999

# Acknowledgements

*W*e received a lot of help from many people and we want to thank all of them again here. We especially appreciate Venerable Yi Jih, Tom Graham, Peggy Willett, Shiow Meei Chen, Lillian Liang, Danny Tam, and Emily Lui for their translation; Rush Glick, Albert Cummings, Carl Ewig, Charles Hardy, Malcolm Koo, Jonathan Iungerich, and Maryrita Hillengas, and Dr. Richard Kimball for their proofreading; Mae Chu and Carol Pen, for preparing the manuscript for publication. The help of these individuals was invaluable and very much appreciated.

# Chapter 1
# The Content and Spirit of
# the Buddha's Light Philosophy

*F*or many years Fo Guang Shan and the Buddha's Light International Association (BLIA) have created a framework, building a system to benefit the world and to save sentient beings. Its methods are practical, and its achievements are visible around the globe. These two Buddhist organizations are like a person's arms, or the wings of a bird. They work together to spread blissful seeds throughout the world.

So, what is the Buddha's Light philosophy? It is the concept of ultimate truth and wholeness. It contains the teaching and guidance needed to increase peace and happiness in the world. The following four points offer some detailed explanations:

## 1. The bodhisattva monastery for Buddha's Light devotees

A monastery is an organization or system that can guide people to Buddhist temples. In this instance, the term bodhisattva is used to differentiate between Shravakas and Pratyeka Buddhas, who are only searching for their own enlightenment. The Buddha established monastic residences and lecture halls in India. In China, during the Tang Dynasty, Ma Zu (709-788 C.E.) established forest monasteries, and Bai Zhang (720-814 C.E.) set up regulations that promoted agricultural-based Chan monasteries. Later, when many masters assembled their disciples to practice Chan and preach the Dharma, their monasteries were called "bodhisattva monasteries." At the end of the Dong Jin Dynasty, Master Dao An (312-385) established a monastery in which to teach during wartime. At the end of the Qing Dynasty, Upasaka Yang Renshan (1837-1911) established Qi Yuan Vihara. He printed sutras and taught classes. In more recent times, Li Pinnan

(1889-1986) established the Lotus Society in Taichung, Taiwan. Others, like master Yuexio (1858-1917), established Huayan University at Shanghai's Hatong Garden. Master Taixu (1889-1947 C.E.) also established a place for bodhisattva learning. They all made an effort to teach the Dharma in order to discover Buddhahood for themselves and to save all sentient beings. All of their centers were called bodhisattva monasteries, but due to prevailing conditions, they were not able to expand their influence.

Fo Guang Shan and the BLIA follow the same bodhisattva spirit of these ancient sages, using compassion to save all sentient beings and purify the world. This has become our responsibility. Working through cultural and educational programs, we focus on creating harmony among groups and individuals. This is the meaning and spirit of both the bodhisattva monastery and the Buddha's Light philosophy.

## 2. Prajna life is Fo Guang Education

Buddhism emphasizes the practice of prajna (wisdom). The sutras mention that prajna is the foremost of the six paramitas. Prajna is the mother of all Buddhas. Like the eyes, prajna guides the other five paramitas toward perfection. Prajna comes from experience in everyday life and apart from life there is no prajna.

The beginning of the *Diamond Sutra* illustrates the Buddha's prajna life. Putting on a robe and holding a bowl represents the Buddha's hands radiating prajna light. Entering Shravasti City to beg for food represents the Buddha's feet radiating prajna light. His actual begging for food represents the Buddha's eyes radiating prajna light. Following a meal, the act of collecting his robe and bowl represents the Buddha's mouth radiating prajna light. Washing his feet and then sitting represents the Buddha's whole body radiating prajna light. The title "World Honored One" represents the Buddha endlessly radiating prajna light. If one understands the *Diamond Sutra* thoroughly, one realizes that there is prajna in daily life. In a Chan monastery, whether wearing clothes, having a meal, chopping wood, carrying water, moving an eyebrow, an eye, or a hand, these are all manifestations of prajna. "The moon in front of a window remains the same, but as soon as there is a plum flower the view will be different." Once there is prajna we can enjoy a carefree life.

Fo Guang Shan and the BLIA are advocates of a *living* Buddhism. We encourage husbands and wives to attend Dharma functions together. We hold activities to bring parents and children together. We emphasize the importance of a joyful family. We emphasize harmony in human relationships. We teach people to develop good habits. These relationships are all in the spirit of a prajna life.

### 3. Harmony in the Dharma realm is the spirit of Buddha's Light

After the Buddha attained enlightenment under the bodhi tree, he taught that all sentient beings possess Buddha Nature. This realization brings hope and light to suffering beings. From this concept develops the idea that all sentient beings are equal, and all Dharma realms are one. These insights are the foundation needed for human beings to reach eternal peace, and they provide guidance that can benefit the entire world.

The Buddha also established equality in the Sangha. He used the Six Harmonies as the guideline for monastic community life. Using "compassion and tolerance" as a guiding principle for harmony among people, he destroyed the differentiation of caste and ethnicity, facilitating the spread of the Dharma in the ten directions. In this way, Buddhism can adapt to different cultures. *beginning* From its inception, Fo Guang Shan has promoted all schools of Buddhism and has followed the principles presented by the four assemblies. The themes for previous annual conferences of the BLIA have been: "Joy and Harmony," "Oneness and Co-existence," "Respect and Tolerance," "Equality and Peace,"

"Wholeness and Freedom," and "Nature and Life." These are all practices and concepts of harmony within the Dharma realm. The BLIA and Fo Guang Shan promote equality between men and women, rich and poor, all vocational levels, and all ethnic groups. We also work to promote harmony among different religions, different schools of Buddhism, traditional and modern thought, and monastics and lay disciples. As we try to apply Buddhism in everyday life, we are making a connection among secular knowledge and Buddhism. Through these ideas and practices we understand that all Dharma realms are one. The concept that all Dharma realms are one is the spirit of Buddha's Light.

### 4. The joys of the world are the spirit of Buddha's Light

Buddhism is a spiritual tradition that promotes joy. The *Lotus Sutra* recounts that the Buddha was born in the human world, renounced his throne, practiced, and became enlightened while in the human world. Avalokiteshvara (Guan Yin) Bodhisattva was enlightened a long time ago, yet returned to save sentient beings from suffering, bringing compassion to this saha (suffering) world. The buddhas and bodhisattvas in the ten directions also practice with joy in order to attain Buddhahood. Maitreya (the Buddha of the future) is called "the Joyful Buddha." Many bodhisattvas have qualities of joy, so one can see that the nature of the Buddha's teaching is joyous. Joyfulness is at the core of Buddhist practice. Fo Guang Shan "gives joyfulness to people", and the BLIA believes that it is vital to realize the truth and use Dharma joy to end all defilements and ignorance. These are the experiences of joy in the human world.

The spirit of Buddha's Light follows both the Buddha's truth, and the example of ancient masters, in order to benefit future generations. We take the bodhisattva monastery and the prajna life as the center of our practice. That "all Dharma realms are one" forms the basis of our thoughts. We take "joy in the human realm" as our practice. Buddha's Light people need the determination to follow this principle so they can benefit both themselves and *all* sentient beings.

**Exercises:**

1. Explain the bodhisattva monastery as the organization and structure for Buddha's Light devotees.
2. How can we experience the *prajna* life?
3. Fo Guang Shan and the BLIA advocate that "all Dharma realms are one." Please explain.
4. Why is "joy in the human realm" the practice of Buddha's Light devotees?

## Chapter 2
## The Teachings of Fo Guang Shan, Its Contemporary Thoughts and Future Missions

*F*rom the onset of the Industrial Revolution, technology has advanced, democracy has emerged, and human rights have been awakened. In recent years, our abundant raw materials have been over-consumed by people's desires. These desires are rapidly depleting the resources of the planet. Wars occur year after year, tainting the purity of human nature. Lives are lost, and human beings face the danger of being consumed by greed, hatred, and ignorance.

What kind of an era are we facing? Around the world, we cheat and lie politically, seeking only to benefit ourselves. Economically, we acquire and form conglomerates. We widen the gap between rich and poor, ethnic groups and religions. We differentiate, suppress, and discriminate against one another. All of these situations reflect our lack of ethical values and ideals.

How can we build a more harmonious and peaceful world? Fo Guang Shan offers the four following proposals:

1. To counter "unfairness," we propose "equanimity."
2. To counter "disrespect for human life," we propose that all people are our priority."
3. To counter the "imbalance in our use of the environment," we propose "environmental protection."
4. To counter the "unreasonableness of human behavior," we propose, "observing the true nature of the universe."

### 1. Equanimity

When we held our Fifth Annual BLIA General Conference in 1996, five thousand representatives gathered in Paris, France. I delivered a talk entitled, *Euanimity in Mutual Respect, Prosperity in Peace* in order to address the idea of equanimity and to advocate peace. My hope was that the delegates, who had come from all over the world, would take this idea back to their countries, thereby aiding the awakening of more people worldwide, and allowing them to come to a mutual under- standing.

How can we have equanimity? Equanimity means that everybody has the same beginning, standing on the same level. It doesn't necessarily mean that everybody should be the same *height*! What does it mean to have the same beginning? For example, a child can only lift a weight of five pounds, but an adult can easily lift up to fifty pounds. Letting a child start with five pounds and an adult with fifty pounds is an example of equanimity of different levels.

True equanimity means the big respect the small, the rich respect the poor, the strong respect the weak, and the higher respect the lower. People must understand the meaning of co-existence. This can be accomplished by understanding that "in the universe, there are tiny seeds, and within a tiny seed, there is also the universe." With such knowledge, you will be able to achieve equanimity amongst diversity, and attain harmony amidst controversy. How can you build a huge machine without screws? How can you construct a skyscraper without sand and stone? If we truly understand the meaning of co-existence, we can see that people rely on one another, and that each person has his or her own distinct character. We can all grow by assisting others. This kind of equanimity is a guarantee of eternal peace.

In summary, peace has to be built from equanimity. Equanimity comes from mutual respect. Communication and understanding are based on the willingness to see the points of view of others. Understanding the diversity of the universe arises from knowing the law of co-existence.

## 2. People are our priority

The fact that the Buddha was born and attained enlightenment in this world indicates the importance of this world, and our precious role as human beings. Nowadays, most people expend their time and energy acquiring material things, using them, and wasting them. Materialism presides over our humanness. Living is no longer joyous, and dying is no longer dignified. The whole world seems driven by the quest for material things.

During the previous millennium, the lack of material goods made people's lives difficult. Today, many people have more material possessions than they need; yet their lives are unfulfilled. Having an abundance of material things can cause people to lose the richness of their spiritual values. It is the emptiness in people's hearts that drives them to live aimlessly.

Our disposable, manufactured items of today are symptomatic. They are not durable, long-lasting, high quality products. They are only something that is used to, we believe, solve an immediate need. These items can be obtained cheaply and instantly, and can also be discarded easily. This type of attitude also affects relationships among family members and friends. Lacking a positive morality, people no longer have the patience to build solid relationships. Divorce, or walking out of a relationship, happens often. "Home" is no longer a *home*. Parents and children are no longer close. They often divert their attention to their pets. When people no longer love their pets, they often discard them like an old shoe. Cats, dogs, insects, fish, and birds are bred and then "abandoned." Such behavior affects the balance of nature and devalues the lives of *all* beings.

Toward the end of the twentieth century, people entered an era that seems to be totally against nature. As we begin the new millennium, people should reflect within themselves, and start anew to emphasize the importance of humankind. Human beings are the center of the Dharma realm. There is hope for humanity only if we care about one another, and treat each other, as we want to be treated ourselves.

## 3. Environmental protection

Today, people destroy nature senselessly, not realizing the seriousness of their wanton destruction.

Air pollution, which has resulted in an increase of carbon dioxide in the atmosphere, traps ultraviolet rays, which causes the greenhouse effect. Tropical forests are bulldozed. Forest fires, both man-made and natural, deeply affect air quality. On each continent, mountains, forests, oceans, and lakes have lost their natural balance. Water is polluted and soil eroded. Some countries do not have adequate sanitation systems to handle waste. Noise in the city, pressures from poor living or working conditions, cancer-causing foods, and other products, are all made by people who have so "wisely" created a prison of their own making. With the earth in such pain, how can people live safely on it?

How do we solve environmental problems? First, we must increase peoples' awareness that the earth is our home. Only through our protection of the earth can we have healthy bodies and minds. Only by not taking our lives, our possessions, our relations, and our blessings for granted, can we be awakened. To protect the environment, we must start by recycling our resources, as well as our ideas. Only then, can we transform defilement into *Bodhi*.

## 4. Observe the true nature of the universe

All three issues mentioned above are the result of people not knowing the natural law of *cause and effect*, and not understanding the law of *co-existence*. The cycle of four seasons (spring, summer, fall, winter), the cycle of life (birth, age, sickness, death), and the cycle of the changes of mind and material things (emerging, existence, decay, dissolution) are all natural.

The Buddhist concept of cause and effect, that everything *coexists*, is a universal truth. In our daily lives, there are some natural and unnatural things. If it is natural, we feel joyous and everything goes smoothly. If it is unnatural, we feel totally exhausted, and we not only hurt ourselves but also others. With feelings, balance and harmony are natural. In communication, consideration and tolerance are natural. In dealing with people, not going against basic principles is natural. In dealing with money, not being in debt is natural. Their opposites are unnatural.

The teachings of Fo Guang Shan advocate humanistic Buddhism. Following the law of co-existence is also natural. In 1998, when we held our seventh annual BLIA convention, the theme of my talk was *Nature and Life*. In my talk I offered four basic points. First, we must understand the laws of nature in order to understand the dignity of life. Second, by treasuring life within nature, we, and all human beings, will experience a higher quality of life. Third, good causes bring good effects. We must restore nature to have a quality life. Fourth, by upgrading the quality of life, the constructive aspects of life emerges, then compassion, kindness, joy, and equanimity will follow.

When we realize that "the green bamboo stalks are wisdom and the yellow flowers are wonderful truth," our lives become true. When we look at all sentient beings with compassion, all are seen to be future Buddhas. We will then naturally walk on the path of enlightenment, and we, along with all sentient beings, will be fulfilled.

**Exercises**

1. Describe the influences and inspiration that the Buddha's Light philosophy exerts upon the development of contemporary thought.

2. Describe the advocacy of equality within the Buddha's Light philosophy

3. Describe the concepts based on the welfare of human beings within the Buddha's Light philosophy.

4. Delineate the environmental protection concepts of the Buddha's Light philosophy.
5. Characterize the laws of nature and dependent origination.
6. Give a detailed description of the effect that the Buddha's Light philosophy can have on the direction and mission of future belief, knowledge, and action.

## Chapter 3
## Harmony between Traditional and Modern Buddhism

*H*istorically cultures develop through ancient wisdom and experience. When we look at the course of history, we see that some cultures have not been able to adapt to contemporary progress. We need modernization. Strictly following tradition is neither right nor wrong, nor is the modern way entirely right or wrong. The best solution is to use the wisdom and experience of tradition to guide modern development. If both traditional and modern ways can work in harmony, there will be universal acceptance.

In the same way, as Buddhism develops, it should not cling to tradition, even though the truth of Buddhism never changes. For example, a method of teaching can be changed to follow current conditions. Traditional Buddhism and modern Buddhism need to be in harmony. There must be cooperation between monastics and lay people, a focus on both practice and understanding, and unity between Buddhism, art, and literature. This is the direction of humanistic Buddhism that is promoted by the Fo Guang Shan Buddhist community.

After many years of effort, there have been positive results in the development of humanistic Buddhism. For example, conservative, traditional Buddhist practices placed an emphasis on asceticism. Today's magnificent modern temples, with air-conditioning, carpeting, electronic equipment, and a comfortable environment, are seemingly contradictory to Buddhist tradition and practice. However, in the extremely blissful world of which the Buddha teaches, the ground is paved with gold, there are seven rows of fences, seven rows of trees, and eight virtuous waters, all magnificent and wonderful.

Today, it is not necessary to be poor or overly frugal to believe in the teachings of Buddhism, and it is not necessary to suffer extreme hardships in order to practice. In fact, Buddhism is a very joyful, rich, and blissful tradition. By promoting Buddhism, we can establish a Pure Land in this world. Modern Buddhism values the importance of wealth (earned responsibily) by emphasizing modern facilities and teaching methods while still finding merit in a peaceful and blissful life.

When the Buddha was teaching, he regularly taught through the use of "supernatural powers." He used himself as an example, by telling stories of his previous lives and the origin of all things. It was evident that he never tired of teaching the Dharma, using many kinds of parables, essays, verses, and poems. He encouraged the promotion and spread of verses by praising the merits of reading, transcribing, and reciting. All of these methods were used to guide sentient beings.

Today's Buddhist disciples should not be disappointed in what the Buddha told us. We can creatively apply tradition through designing and creating charts, flyers, and posters, and publishing newspapers and magazines. We can also use poems, proverbs, and wise words to teach the Dharma. With modern technology, we can use radio and television, computers, and the Internet. This is similar to the way that the Buddha, who used his "long tongue" to teach, spread the Dharma everywhere.

In the past, Buddhism emphasized the importance of making pilgrimages, traveling, and visiting. In the Buddhist sutras it mentions how celestial beings, after a meal, do walking meditation and offer flowers to other Buddha lands. Today, Chinese Buddhism values the importance of pilgrimages to sacred sites, visits with monastics at temples, meditation, and discussion to enhance one's practice. Through these methods one can befriend all and broaden one's views. This is a modern presentation of traditional Buddhism.

In the Buddha's time, celestial beings spread flowers and made music. They also made offerings of songs and dances to attract people to Dharma functions. When the Buddha taught at Vulture Peak, an audience of millions listened to his talk. These methods are still praised by modern people. The Buddha gave teachings as well as joy. He was skillful in using many different teaching methods.

Today, at a Buddhist ordination, the masters and preceptees use flowers to invite all of the Buddhas of the ten directions. In Chinese Buddhist history, Yu Shan Buddhist music and verses, along with the dancing gestures of celestial beings, aided people in feeling joyful. Today, Fo Guang Shan and the BLIA teach devotees to use Buddhist music and dancing to praise the Buddhas in all worlds. Today's audiences appreciate the harmony between Buddhist music and dance.

In the past, the Buddhist monastic communities focused on the spirit of the principle of the Six Harmonies. Our modern Fo Guang Shan Buddhist organization uses the Dharma as the central theme. Our emphasis is on following the Dharma rather than a leader. We also emphasize following the system, using teamwork, the rotation of duties, and the establishment of different personnel levels. The rules of the Sangha are compatiable with all of these modern administrative procedures. This is not contradictory to traditional Buddhism.

Buddhism values the cultivation of the inner mind. "All of the Dharma that the Buddha taught was used to heal all kinds of minds. If there are not all kinds of minds, of what use is the Dharma?" One modern method of purifying the mind is psychotherapy.

In traditional Buddhist teaching, the Buddha promoted the equality of all castes. Today we include monastics, lay people, and the four assemblies into the same family. All work together in harmony.

Modern society emphasizes enterprise management, investment, and the management of personal finances. In the past, Shakyamuni Buddha valued the way of running a business, and also stressed the importance of both saving and being generous. Once we have money, how are we going to manage it? In the same sutra, there are four verses explaining money management. These verses refer to giving, saving, investing, and daily usage. One should give one-tenth, save two-tenths, invest three-tenths, and use four-tenths for daily life.

Today, many people place an emphasis on family life. In the past, the Buddha emphasized cultivation for lay people. Even though Upasaka Vimalakirti had a wife and children, he continued to practice pure deeds. Many people also emphasize relationships between parents and children, husbands and wives, relatives and friends, employers and employees, and teachers and students. In the *Sigalovada Sutra*, the Buddha gave very useful advice about how to get along in different relationships.

There is no actual difference between traditional Buddhism and modern Buddhism. In fact, all of these teachings are the Buddha's teachings. The teachings give guidance, joy, and benefit. In the development of Fo Guang Shan, and in the establishment of the BLIA, our main purpose has been to apply traditional Buddhism to modern life.

**Exercises:**

1. Explain the significance of harmony between modern and traditional culture.

2. Give two examples to show how Buddhism may harmonize traditional and modern ways of teaching the Dharma.

3. Use two examples to descrive how Fo Guang Shan harmonizes traditional and modern life.

# Chapter 4
## The Development and Direction of the Buddha's Light philosophy

A Buddha's Light Philosophy is based on the following four points:

1. Communicate in the Ten Directions at all times.
2. Compassion as the foundation, upaya as the method.
3. Buddhism as the body, secular knowledge as the tool.
4. The whole universe is one family, I am one with all sentient beings.

A brief explanation of each point follows.

### 1. Communicate in the ten directions at all times

From a spatial perspective, this means that our original Buddha Nature radiates in the ten directions. The Dharma body exists everywhere. From the viewpoint of time, Buddha Nature has no birth and no death; it is permanent and unchanging. By applying this truth, we can understand the relationship between others and ourselves. We can also comprehend the rising and falling of conditions. We awaken to the coming and going of time and space. From this knowledge, we can develop our inner treasure.

People often ask, "How does your management system work with a Buddhist organization that has so many people and so many complicated activities? How can everyone work together and get along harmoniously?" The answer relies on the principle of communicating in the ten directions at all times. By practicing communication in the ten directions, one's viewpoint can be expanded. Communication opens our hearts, and broadens our perspective. When we realize that the minds of sentient beings have no boundaries of either nation or space, there can be no distinction based on color or ethnicity. When we see all sentient beings as one, then we are perfectly willing to contribute to their Buddhahood.

Communicating in the ten directions at all times is the golden principle of how to be a good person, and how to get along with leaders and management. It is the best way to build a successful career, and serves a fundamental role in group development. The Buddha's Light philosophy is based on humanity. The path of future development should emphasize the path to perfection in everyday life, purification of the body and mind, the establishment of family ethics to enhance harmonious relationships between people, and respect for nature and life. These practices follow the principle of communication in the ten directions at all times. We should open the gate for everyone.

## 2. Compassion as the foundation, Upaya as the way

Compassion is the root, or foundation of Dharma teaching. If we lose compassion in saving sentient beings, then there is no Buddhahood to achieve. Upaya (skillful means) is applied when teaching. If we are not able to apply upaya with dedication and discipline, we are unable to complete our duty. The *Vimala-kirti-nirdesa Sutra* says, "Compassion is the father, upaya is the mother." Compassion and upaya are the best means to lead sentient beings towards the Buddha's wisdom. Upaya has many facets. Through the six senses, upaya is used to guide us to the path. For example, some people enter the path by seeing a magnificent Buddha Hall, while others enter the path upon hearing a drum and bell. Some people enter the path because they smell the fragrant incense in the Buddha Hall, while others enter the path because they taste a wonderful meal in the dining hall. Some people enter the path through bowing and making pilgrimages, while others enter the path because they realize the impermanence of life.

There are many ways that guide sentient beings to the path. Not only may one be guided by Dharma functions, but also it may occur through literature, art, books, paintings, vegetarian food or tea. All can guide people to Buddhism. The BLIA has designed various activities to appeal to different people. Some examples are: Dharma discussion groups, Dharma protector's seminars, meditation classes, and Sunday classes for adults and children. Our programs benefit all Dharma practitioners, young and old, male and female. Providing a multitude of activities can be akin to Avalokitesvara (Guan Yin) Bodhisattva, who manifests in a myriad of forms to best teach the Dharma to each sentient being.

The development and direction of the Buddha's Light philosophy uses boundless upaya. We offer sentient beings compassion and joy by leading them to practice wholesome deeds and to increase their morality. Using compassion as the foundation, and upaya as the way, we emulate the spirit of Avalokiteshvara Bodhisattva/Guan Yin who manifests in different forms, travels to different lands, saves sentient beings, and uses endless compassion with boundless upaya to accomplish her teachings.

### 3. Buddhism as the body, knowledge as the tool

With respect to modern technology and culture, all is subject to change and needs to be constantly upgraded. We should apply Buddhism in a modern way, by adapting to current changes and finding new solutions. This method allows "Buddhism to be the guide and knowledge the tool." Buddhism is in this world. It cannot be found apart from it. We should harmonize Buddhism and knowledge. Harmonizing Buddhism and knowledge is an important direction for the future development of the Buddha's Light philosophy.

The purpose of Buddhism is to relieve suffering and to give joy. The function of Buddhism is upaya and harmony. For example, when the Buddha was young, he learned many things. After he became a monk, he visited different teachers from other religions. The Buddha understood both knowledge and the

Dharma, which allowed him to teach different kinds of people. To different beliefs, he gave different responses, thus ending the suffering of body and mind.

Modern society is constantly faced with all kinds of issues. Buddhists should not run away and ignore them, nor should they forget about the suffering of all sentient beings. We should give proper consideration to economic issues, international conditions, human rights, living conditions, educational reform, conflicts between ethnic groups, environmental protection, family violence, in vitro fertilization, organ donation, feng shui, and fortune telling.

With Buddhism as the guide, and using current knowledge as the tool, we can combine conditioned genesis with psychological counseling to help people in understanding how to respect life and treasure the human body. We can teach people the concept of cause and effect, and assist them in understanding how to treasure their good fortune, and how to befriend all with humility and gratitude.

We have invited experts to present papers on the concept of rebirth, to let people know that life is endless, and how birth and death are in reality one. We take conditioned genesis and the middle path as our guide, and the Four Guiding Principles and the Six Paramitas as our tools. We accept all secular dharmas.

According to the *Avatamsaka Sutra*, there was a young man named Sudhana-sresthi-daraka who visited fifty-three teachers and studied all kinds of worldly knowledge. He learned astrology, geography, medicine, mathematics, navigation, and trade. After accumulating such knowledge, it was possible for him to enter the Dharma realm. This story makes the point of not neglecting the value of worldly knowledge, secular teaching and modern technology, which are not necessarily incompatible with spiritual values.

**4. The whole universe is one family; I am one with all sentient beings.**

In Confucianism, the goal is to have a joyful universe and a peaceful world. Dr. Sun Yat-sen also established a new country, the Republic of China, based on the belief that the universe belongs to all people. Buddhism maintains the belief that the whole universe is one family, and that all people are one. Following this thought, it is possible for us to establish a Pure Land on this earth.

Traditional Chinese culture espouses the idea that we should "not only take care of our own elders, but also take care of the elders of others; not only nourish the youth of our own generation but also the youth of other generations." In Buddhism we not only protect human rights, but also emphasize the equality of all sentient beings. All sentient beings possess Buddha Nature. Because Buddhism values the equality of all sentient beings, we believe everyone has the potential to be a future Buddha. By thinking in this way, we can transcend the barriers of nationality, ethnicity, and species allowing the whole universe to be one family. Therefore, by resolving differences, we can reach the point where all beings are one.

If we can accept the whole universe as one family, then we can accept the differences among all bengs and not reject any. For example, our eyes can appreciate natural beauty, our ears can listen to the birds singing and insects humming, and our nose can breathe fresh air to provide the blood with oxygen. The pores in our skin, although small, can aid the body's circulation. Buddhism emphasizes teamwork. Don't look down on any sentient being; don't miss any small condition.

The development and direction of the BLIA promotes the ideal of the whole universe as one family. We take this concept as the starting point of our practice, and encourage everyone to be open-minded in order to become a global being. We should protect nature and treasure our resources, taking the position that all beings are one. When we enlighten ourselves and awaken others, we elevate our own life. By holding the right views of ourselves and other sentient beings, the light of compassion will radiate throughout the world, and we will improve society.

**Exercises:**

1. Describe the concept of the ten directions in space, and the three lifetimes in time, as it applies to the development and direction of the Buddha's Light philosophy.

2. Why is it said that "compassion is the foundation, upaya is the way" is the sublime method of spreading the Dharma and saving all beings?

3. Describe the importance of "the Dharma as the essence and secular knowledge as application" in the development and direction of the Buddha's Light philosophy.

4. How is the idea of "the whole universe is one family and I am one with all sentient beings" used to establish the ideals of the development and direction of the Buddha's Light philosophy?

# Chapter 5
# The Foundation of the BLIA

*B*uddhism is for both monastics and lay people. However, in the past, traditional Buddhism focused mostly on monastics. If the vast contributions that are made by devotees cannot be acknowledged, there will be a breach between Buddhism and the society within which it exists. The direction of the BLIA flows "from monastic to lay followers, from the temple to society, from study to teaching, from tranquility to action, from disciple to teacher, from local to global" in order to adapt to the needs of the times.

Although the official inauguration ceremony of the BLIA was held on May 16, 1992, the actual history of the establishment of the BLIA goes back to August 10, 1990, when the first organizational meeting was held in Taipei, Taiwan. On that date, 108 organizers were in attendance. During the meeting, several important decisions were made, including the name of organization (Buddha's Light International Association), its objectives, and the by-laws and obligations of the organization. This framework became the focal point for future goals and directed the organization's development.

Nine days later, on August 19th, the BLIA registered with the Ministry of the Interior of the Republic of China and applied for permission to organize. By September 24th, the BLIA received a notice from the Ministry of the Interior that it was approved. From then on, all plans became a reality.

On November 3rd, we held a second organizational meeting, during which thirty-one people were elected to the organizing committee. This committee unanimously elected Venerable Master Hsing Yun as their director. At the same time, all who were present were invited to join.

On February 3rd, 1991, the BLIA of the Republic of China was formally inaugurated at Sun Yat-sen Memorial Hall in Taipei. The inauguration drew more than 5,000 representatives who elected Venerable Master Hsing Yun as the president of the BLIA Republic of China Chapter. During the ceremony, the President of the Republic of China, Lee Teng-hui, presented his congratulatory message. Many other dignitaries were also present at this event, which was acclaimed as the most important inauguration for a religious-based organization in many years.

Following the establishment of the BLIA in the Republic of China and the United States, other countries soon organized chapters. Canada, Brazil, Argentina, Australia, New Zealand, France, England, and Germany were among the earliest countries to develop BLIA chapters. The Philippines, Malaysia, Japan, South Africa, and Hong Kong soon followed. Eventually, more than sixty countries joined the BLIA, and by September 1991, we held the first planning meeting of the BLIA to began building communications between chapters, and a month later at Fo Guang Shan, a second organizational meeting was attended by representatives from all over the world.

Every activity has to have all conditions come together at just the right moment to become complete. On May 16, 1992, the BLIA celebrated its grand opening at the Los Angeles Music Center. More than 4,000 representatives from forty-five countries attended this historic meeting. At the same time, we held the first membership conference and, once again, all members who were present elected Venerable Master Hsing Yun as president. Five vice presidents from Japan, Hong Kong, Australia and Sri Lanka were also elected. The election results displayed the international character and harmony of the BLIA.

The BLIA is somewhat different from secular social organizations in that its members share the same beliefs. They are not only searching for liberation for themselves and others, but for the development of their wisdom. They are united in their goal to establish a harmonious society that promotes peace and mutual respect. It is an organization dedicated "to the betterment of oneself and others, and to the idea of living in oneness and coexistence."

Since its inception, BLIA has taken education, culture, practice, and service as its primary objectives. Its establishment has provided lay devotees with an opportunity to give of themselves and to participate in Buddhist charity work. Teachers of the Dharma and practitioners of Mahayana thus plant positive seeds in their cultures. Practices such as holding the International Buddhist Sangha Conference, bringing together the Southern, Northern, Sutric, and Tantric traditions, and unifying monastics with lay people are among the "seeds" that the BLIA plants. The BLIA forms a true international community, which transcends nationality, ethnicity, and tradition.

The BLIA is now recognized throughout the world. Although it has only been in existence for less than ten years, it has more than 130 associations and 1,000 sub-chapters, (including twenty-seven non-Chinese groups), with a membership of over one million. There are more than thirty countries preparing to establish BLIA branches. In South Africa, more than 100,000 people have expressed an interest in becoming members.

The growth of BLIA is a manifestation of the international character of Fo Guang Shan. The BLIA has achieved its goal of the internationalization of Buddhism and has brought Buddhism into a new era. A new milestone for the future development of Buddhism has been reached!

**Exercises:**
1. Describe the origins of BLIA.
2. What contributions have been made up until now by the BLIA towards bettering societies and nations?
3. What are the characteristics of the BLIA?

## Chapter 6
# The Purpose and Principles of the BLIA

*O*ne of the most important aspects of any organization is its objectives. Objectives not only define the purpose of an organization, they help set goals for each member to work toward. For Buddhist devotees of the BLIA, and its worldwide community of citizens, the Four Guiding Principles of the BLIA can be stated as follows.

1. The BLIA is founded on a belief in the teachings of the Buddha, on respect for the Triple Gem, and on the interest in spreading the Dharma for the benefit of all sentient beings.

2. As BLIA members, we should advocate a living Buddhism that seeks to create a Pure Land in this world.

3. As BLIA members, we should revere the practices given to us by the Buddha, and we should fully develop ourselves by practicing the Three Learnings: morality, meditation, and wisdom.

4. As BLIA members, we each vow to cultivate a broad-minded character, one that is capable of embracing all cultures and societies. We should always be willing to open our hearts and do whatever we can to aid others.

"Belief in the teachings of the Buddha, and respect for the Triple Gem of Buddhism," explains how BLIA members can achieve Buddhahood. The Triple Gem is the core of our belief. The fundamental practices of BLIA members are to respect the Triple Gem, teach Buddhism, and benefit all sentient beings.

The sixth Chan Patriarch Huineng said, "The Dharma is to be found in this world, and to leave this world to search for the Dharma is as futile as searching for a rabbit with horns." Buddhism is a religion based on humanism. Buddhism cannot be separated from life. If we retreat from life, there will be no way to find Buddhism. The BLIA follows the Buddha's teachings by promoting a living Buddhism. We advocate the family as a "monastery" for practice. Buddhism cannot be contradictory to our lives. Husbands and wives should not be enemies. On the other hand, the bodhi couple can support each other along the Buddhist path. We should not be at odds with our children. The more responsibly created money that we have, the more we can follow Buddhist careers. Money, in itself, is not a "poisonous snake." Profit is not intrinsically evil. A respected reputation and generous donations can inspire us in our progress to emulate the sages. If we put Buddhism into practice in this world, then we can benefit others with compassion. We will be able to transform this saha world into a Buddha's Light Pure Land.

We need to understand the proper way of spreading the Dharma to the world. There is a saying, "There are many expedient ways, but the goal is the same." In Buddhism, there are many different teachings. Buddhism is divided into five levels that are called the Five Yanas. These five levels include the Human Vehicle where we practice the Three Refuges and the Five Precepts. The Heavenly Vehicle is where we practice the Ten Wholesome Deeds and meditation. The Shravaka Vehicle is where we practice the Four Noble Truths. The Pratyeka Buddha Vehicle is where we practice the truth of conditioned genesis. A bodhisattva practices the awakening and freeing of all sentient beings from delusion. Although the Six Perfections and all the practices of the Five Yanas have many facets, the heart of any practice is discipline, meditation, and wisdom.

Because BLIA members accept the responsibility to teach the Dharma to benefit all sentient beings, they first need to observe the precepts, practice meditation, and realize wisdom. Through the completion of the Three Learnings, one can fully develop one's character. The transformation of one's "illusion of self" is the ultimate accomplishment of the Buddhist path. BLIA members should harmonize with the Five Vehicles, and take the

Three Learnings and Six Perfections as their guides for practice. We should develop an open-minded international view, without distinctions based on geography, ethnicity, nationality, or religion. Throughout the world, through culture and education, BLIA members should make every effort to benefit all sentient beings. By benefiting sentient beings through culture, the Dharma can reach far and touch every corner of the earth.

Only through education can we really purify our minds. From the objectives of the BLIA, we can see that members carry the responsibility of spreading the Dharma and benefiting all sentient beings. Members have the compassion necessary to free the world from all suffering, moral discipline, and they value community.

Buddhism has always embodied universalism, the concept that geographic limitations do not exist. Buddhism belongs to the world, and to all people. So, BLIA members should stand locally and think globally. They should plant bodhi seeds on every continent, allowing the Dharma to be introduced worldwide.

One important duty of the BLIA is to carry Buddhism from the temple to society, from the monastic to the lay follower, and into family life as well as practicing while working to support oneself and one's family. In order to spread the Dharma, BLIA members should learn to write well, use computers, and publish. To beautify the monastery, we should learn flower arrangement, decoration, and architecture. To spread the Dharma, we should learn and use different methods of teaching.

Through all types of activities, the BLIA provides members with an opportunity to participate in Buddhist practice. In this world members will begin to increase their merit and wisdom through mindfulness in their everyday lives. On the spiritual level, we can provide members with much assistance. We can aid them in solving their difficulties and settle their frustrations.

To increase the thoroughness and breadth of their beliefs, BLIA members should join Buddhist discussions and associate with teachers. We should not let feng shui, fortunetellers, and horoscopes control us. Mysterious and negative beliefs will not sway us if we constantly develop right understanding, right views, right practice, and the ability to discriminate between right and wrong. Members may take the opportunity to improve themselves, and they can show others what they have learned, completing the Bodhisattva practice to benefit both oneself and others.

The BLIA not only has clear objectives and goals, we promote vows that are rich in foresight, spirit, and content. BLIA members should adopt the Mahayana Bodhisattva spirit. We will then be inspired to have kindness, compassion, joy, and equanimity, to practice the Six Perfections, and to possess the determination to be the manifestation of the Buddha in this world.

Our teacher, Shakyamuni Buddha, taught in India over 2,500 years ago. Today, Buddhists must clarify his lessons, and allow the Dharma to reach far and wide. When this occurs, the Buddha's Light will shine everywhere, and Dharma waters will flow forever. These are the objectives and goals of the BLIA and all its members.

**Exercises:**

1. What are the guiding principles that created the BLIA?
2. What are the ideals regarding the establishment of the BLIA?
3. What are the basic practices of members of the BLIA?
4. How do members of the BLIA actualize Buddhism in their everyday lives?
5. How do members of the BLIA spread the Dharma?

## Chapter 7
# The Meaning of the BLIA Anthem

*T*he BLIA is an international Buddhist organization. The BLIA Anthem should be sung at the end of a gathering to reaffirm our goals and direction. The lyrics of the anthem are as follows:

> *Our objective is to spread the Dharma.*
> *Our belief is to tell right from wrong.*
> *Our inspiration is the four Bodhisattvas.*
> *Our sincere hope is to build a Pure Land.*
> *We benefit society, broadening our horizons;*
> *We exist as one, embracing the world.*
> *Listen! Our pledge is that the Buddha's Light*
> *Shines everywhere.*
> *The Dharma waters flow forever.*

The Buddha was reborn in this saha world to teach, to guide people toward enlightenment, and to aid them in understanding the Dharma. The BLIA includes both monastic and lay followers. Both groups work together for the purpose of achieving the Buddha's path and continuing the Buddha's teachings. Monastics should follow the Buddha's example by teaching the Dharma. The main duty of lay followers is to support and preserve the Dharma. To offer Buddhism in order to reach deep into people's minds for the attainment of ultimate peace and happiness has become the aim of the BLIA.

In order to spread the Dharma to benefit sentient beings, one needs to have right understanding. The point of right understanding is to free ourselves from the cycle of birth and death. It is also a basic requirement in learning and practicing Buddhism. Generally, today's society displays a lack of right understanding. Incorrect views and negative thoughts are everywhere.

They hinder creating a wholesome atmosphere in society. Through the practice of right understanding, BLIA members can emulate the compassion of Avalokitesvara (Guan Yin) Bodhisattva who saves sentient beings by hearing their cries for help, emulate the wisdom of Manjusri Bodhisattva who opens the treasure within ourselves, emulate the great practice of Samantabhadra Bodhisattva who practices all kinds of Dharma, and emulate Ksitigarbha Bodhisattva who saves all sentient beings from suffering. Let every member of the BLIA become a manifestation of these four Bodhisattvas. Let them share the duty of teaching the right path that destroys the negative and benefits all sentient beings.

Equality and compassion are characteristics of Buddhism. Coexistence and oneness embody equality and compassion. The *Avatamsaka Sutra* says we should free all sentient beings from suffering and not be concerned about our own happiness. The BLIA is an organization that focuses on social causes. We respect the rights of all sentient beings, with unconditional loving kindness and with great compassion, because all sentient beings are one. The mind, the Buddha, and sentient beings are not different. We live on this earth; therefore we should consider ourselves global beings who can coexist with oneness. We should emphasize awareness of the fact that all sentient beings and all Buddhas are equal, arhats and ordinary people are equal, theory and practice are equal and you and I are equal. Furthermore, to benefit society, we should make an effort to care for the poor, the weak, the old, the young, and those in need. With the wonderful Dharma, we should free sentient beings who are suffering. All Buddhas have their own Pure Lands. Although this saha world is full of distruction and negativity, through the Buddha's pure mind, this world can also become a Pure Land.

Everyone can practice the Six Perfections and the Four Guiding Principles, thereby befriending all, changing feelings of hatred and jealousy into those of respect and tolerance, and replacing attitudes of competition with joy and happiness for the benefit of others. If the sensations that we receive through our six senses are true, wholesome, and beautiful, and all of our friends are good people, then this saha world will become the Buddha's Light Pure Land.

We hope that by following our objectives, beliefs, and spirit, we can promote Buddhism in a universal way. At the same time, we can inspire our subchapters to work toward the establishment of a peaceful, happy, harmonious, and blissful society, to work for world peace, and to positively influence the future direction of the world. In this way the BLIA will always be able to follow conditions and spread the Dharma. In this way, Buddha's Light Dharma waters will flow on all six continents forever.

**Exercises:**

1. Describe the meaning of the BLIA Anthem.
2. How do members of the BLIA emulate the Four Great Bodhisattvas?

## Chapter 8
## Talks on Major BLIA Themes

*I*n the present era, mass communication is readily available, and citizens of this planet can travel around the world as they please. Buddhism can break away from its past by coming out of the forest and entering society. This can be accomplished through expanding the functions of temples, and serving the community through involvement with families, nations, and the world at large.

Over the years, BLIA members have sought to promote humanistic Buddhism. They have worked to modernize and develop the literature of Buddhism and to make it more accessible to all people. To achieve its goals, the BLIA has held an annual general conference nearly every year since 1992. At each of these conferences, a "theme talk" was presented for the spiritual guidance and direction for future goals of BLIA members.

*Joy and Harmony:*
> *This speech was given in 1992 at the Los Angeles Music Center.*

In the world, which we live, virtually everybody wants to have wealth, love, knowledge, and power. But these things, as desirable as they may seem, will probably only bring defilement and distruction. As a matter of fact, it is far better to have joy and harmony. It is our hope that everyone will work with joy, live with joy, face adversity with joy, and benefit others with joy. We hope for everything to be in harmony.

Followers of the Mahayana and Theravada schools need to be unified with the sutric and the tantric, self and others, theory and practice. There should also be harmony among all ethnic groups. Therefore, the BLIA wants to spread joy worldwide, enabling all people to be in complete harmony, regardless of ethnicity or nationality. By understanding that there are differences in similari ties and similarities in differences, people will be able to live with one another in a spirit of peace and cooperation.

***Oneness and Coexistence:***
***This speech was given in 1993 at Lingko Coliseum, Taiwan and 1994 at UBC, Vancouver, Canada.***
"Oneness" means equanimity. It also means equality and tolerance. Although there are differences in gender, age, strength, and intelligence among all sentient beings, they are all the same with regards to their pure Buddha Nature. The moment that the Buddha was enlightened, he proclaimed: "Every sentient being has the same wisdom as the Buddha." The concept of equanimity proposed by the Buddha promotes equality between sentient beings and the Buddha, between bodhisattvas and ordinary persons, between theory and practice, and between self and others.

"Coexistence" requires the vision of compassion. This means that we must have compassion in order to be in harmony with others.

All sentient beings in this Dharma realm rely on each other for existence and prosperity. Coexistence is what Buddhism advocates: "Be kind to all sentient beings, even those whom you don't know; have compassion toward others as if they are yourself." This type of compassion is an example of an untainted kindness and tolerance that goes beyond "self" or "others." At work, people should treat each other as if no "rank" separates them. In daily life, people should not calculate gain or loss at each step. Coexistence requires respect and tolerance for each other. Coexistence and co-prosperity are basic components of nature.

We all live on planet earth. We should forsake our own self-righteous opinions and discriminations, in order to benefit one another. We should promote the idea of oneness and advocate the principle of equanimity. We should use coexistence to enhance the spirit of kindness, compassion, joy, and equanimity. In this way, we will make our world a Pure Land of peace and joy.

## Respect and Tolerance:

*This speech was given in 1995 at the International Conference Center in Sydney, Australia.*

Respect and tolerance are especially important in a society that is permeated by advanced technology and transportation. We must respect the freedom of others, upholding the five precepts and not giving in to aggression. We respect the value of life by offering compassion in place of killing. Buddhists respect the possessions of others by promoting sharing in place of selfishness. Finally, we respect nature and protect the environment by practicing conservation in place of destruction. In addition, we should use our "non-self" awareness to feel less estranged from people who seem to be different from us.

Understanding that there is no distinction between the "clean" and "unclean", we will be able to preserve the dignity of those who are physically or mentally challenged. Having the wisdom to treat both our friends and our enemies in the same way, we will be able to tolerate any harm they might do to us. Understanding that the sage and the ordinary person are basically the same, we will be able to tolerate unintentional mistakes. If we all treat our professions with respect, care for others with a spirit of joy, and benefit others with tolerance, then transforming the world we live in into a Pure Land will be something to anticipate in the near future.

## Equanimity and Peace:

*This speech was given in 1996 at Conference Center, Paris.*

Equanimity and peace are two sides of the same coin. True equanimity does not try to make everybody the same. True peace cannot be achieved by threats or by force. We must purify our minds and achieve mutual understanding in order to harvest the joy of equanimity and peace. One can build mutual respect on a daily basis. When we place ourselves in the shoes of others, our respect for those who are less fortunate than us should increase. We can use compassion and tolerance to erase our discriminations, so as to live peacefully and prosperously.

*Wholeness and Freedom:*
  *This speech was given in 1997 at Hong Kong International Trade & Exhibition Centre.*

In our lives, many things are imperfect, such as a separation from loved ones, experiencing ups and downs, and our having love/hate relationships. All of these bring sadness to our lives. In Buddhism, the highest level of ultimate Nirvana, eternal joy and purity, is the true Pure Land. "Perfection" means: the most natural and the most beautiful. Perfection is a level that everyone wants to attain. We should learn to cultivate our minds to be tolerant, to be content to learn wisdom in dealing with others, and to acquire stability in society. We should also strive to attain harmony in the family, achieve health in mind and body, and attain liberation of the self. In this way, we experience the perfection and ease of this world.

*Nature and Life:*
  *This speech was given in 1998 at Regal Constellation Hotel, Toronto.*

The ways of nature form the reality of our world. The cycle of the seasons- spring, summer, autumn, and winter- and the life cycle of all sentient beings- birth, sickness, aging, and death- are all natural. There is life if something is natural; there is growth, if it is natural; there are ways, if it is natural; there are truth and beauty, if it is natural.

Buddhism's essence is nature, and it emphasizes the human mind and human nature. Only when we respect and flow with nature will we then liberate ourselves and become free. The true meaning of life is not whether something is still breathing; it depends on whether it has value.

Besides human life, all matter and natural resources that are useful to people and contribute to mankind should be viewed as having a "life." Therefore, Fo Guang Shan uses the theme "Nature and Life" to encourage people to experience the life of nature and the nature of life. It is hoped that by raising people's awareness, they will then treasure the breath of life and merge with the universal.

If everybody in the world can live their lives by following the rule of "Nature and Life," they will have tranquility in their hearts, their families will be happy and harmonious, and society will be peaceful. This is the world that Buddhism promises to bring.

**Exercises:**

1. How can one practice "Joy and Harmony" in daily living?

2. Describe the conscious spirit of "Oneness and Coexistence."

3. How do we extend the attitude of "Respect and Tolerance" toward establishing a Pure Land?

4. How can we attain true equality among people and peace on earth?

5. How do we transcend the pain and impermanence of worldly life for universal "Wholeness and Freedom?"

6. Describe the relationship between "Nature and Life."

## Chapter 9
# Buddha's Light Samadhi

Since the ultimate goal of every Buddhist is to achieve liberation, every BLIA member should practice Buddha's Light Samadhi daily. The daily practice of Buddha's Light Samadhi enables members to be in harmony with the Triple Gem and all sentient beings.

Absolute mindfulness will be achieved with the improvement of the Three Karmas: (body, speech, mind). Practicing the Three Wisdoms: (listening, contemplation, cultivation), and the Three Learnings: (precepts, concentration, wisdom), will improve the Three Karmas. Other aspects of this practice include the making of vows, pure practice, repentance, and transference of merit. If all Buddhists practice accordingly, they will be able to perfect the practice of the Six Paramitas within their own minds, while establishing a Pure Land on this earth.

Samadhi is a profound state of concentration, mindfulness, and absorption. The practice simply consists of focusing on one subject. When Samadhi is achieved, one will be able to both enhance one's wisdom and discover one's own true nature. *Samadhi* is both unifying and liberating.

Chapter Nine of the *Vairocana Sutra* describes four characteristics of Samadhi:

1. *Equality*: The mind, the Buddha, and all sentient beings are equal.
2. *Vow*: Making a vow to practice the Four Immeasurable States of Mind and Four Guiding Principles, in order to benefit all sentient beings.
3. *Eradication of obstructions*: Protection of the mind through using the precepts for the eradication of all negative karmas of the past, present, and future.

4. *Awareness*: Constant awareness of the reality within and
without, in order to control laziness and complacency.

Buddha's Light Samadhi focuses on the Dharma realms of the
universe, and progresses to the practice of the Three Karmas of
body, speech, and mind. Consistent practice opens one's mind
to embrace sentient beings in all Dharma realms. The following
sections are recommendations regarding the practice of Buddha's
Light Samadhi.

## 1. Making vows

The practice of karma of the body begins with paying homage
to the Triple Gem, chanting, and bowing. A deep sense of respect
and aspiration should develop from within the heart in order to
integrate with the pure Triple Gem. The twelve vows are described as follows.

### The First Vow

In the entire universe, there is no one like the Buddha. In all Ten
Realms, there is no one who can compare to the Buddha. In all
that I see in this world, there is no one equal to the Buddha.

### The Second Vow

Through countless ages of time, the Buddha's wonderful Dharma
has been difficult to find. Now that I have seen and heard it, I vow
to accept the Tathagata's Dharma.

### The Third Vow

The members of the Sangha are pure, clothed in the robes of the
Tathagata; they are examples of virtue in both the heavenly realms
on and earth. By upholding the precepts, they achieve liberation.

### The Fourth Vow

With singleness of mind, I bow before all Buddhas, the awakened
and the noble, who abide throughout the universe.

**The Fifth Vow**
With singleness of mind, I bow before the Dharma, which is completely pure, and abides throughout the universe.

**The Sixth Vow**
With singleness of mind, I bow before the Sangha members who are compassionate and joyful, and who abide throughout the universe.

**The Seventh Vow**
I pay homage to this saha world, to the master of the heavenly realms and of earth, the master of the Three Realms, the compassionate leader of all sentient beings, our founding master, the World-Honored One, Shakyamuni Buddha.

**The Eighth Vow**
I pay homage to the Tushita Heaven Realm, to the Eka-jati-prati-buddha, and to the next Buddha, Maitreya Bodhisattva.

**The Ninth Vow**
I pay homage to the Great Compassionate One, who relieves all suffering and hardship and who answers all calls for help, Avalokitesvara (Guan Yin) Bodhisattva.

**The Tenth Vow**
I pray for world peace, human joy, liberation of both mind and body, and the prosperity of the Dharma.

**The Eleventh Vow**
I pray for sentient beings in all Dharma realms, for my parents of many lifetimes, my teachers, friends, enemies, relatives, those to whom I owe debts, and my ancestors; may they all be reborn in the Pure Land.

**The Twelfth Vow**

I vow not to only awaken and free myself, not to pursue the blessings of heaven and earth for my benefit, and not to follow the Shravaka path or the Pratyekabuddha path alone. I vow not to become lost in routine, or in the worship of Bodhisattvas, but I vow to rely completely on the highest Yana, which is the Bodhi mind. I vow to attain anuttara-samyak-sambodhi with all sentient beings.

## 2. Chanting

This method is compatible with speech karma. Chanting suits every practitioner, be they scholar or those with a limited education. With today's busy lifestyle, chanting is also suitable for any place and any time. Since there are four methods of chanting, I would suggest practicing each method and interchanging them in order to balance one's mind and to achieve the harmonious middle path. The four methods of chanting are:

A. *Chanting with joy*: Wishing to be reborn in the Pure Land, to be liberated from rebirths, and to abide with sages in a golden land of treasures, while listening to the teaching of the Dharma by the Buddha, thus filling one's whole being with Dharma joy.

B. *Chanting with sadness*: Contemplating the suffering and pain of being reborn from beginningless time, with only the compassionate Buddha to rely on for deliverance.

C. *Chanting with emptiness*: Contemplating the transience of existing in a world in which the physical body, composed of the four gross elements and five aggregates, can easily disintegrate. Only by chanting the Buddha's name can we blend with the whole universe.

D. *Chanting with truthfulness*: Chanting requires the co-ordination of body, speech, and mind. While visualizing images of the Buddha illuminating the universe, and while chanting clearly and truthfully one must be respectful and devout.

## 3. Meditation

In this practice one's mind is focused on compassion. Practicing well enables one to be at peace with everyone and everything, without hatred or worry. Meditation also fills one with endless joy and an abundant accumulation of merits. There are two levels of practice:

A. *Vow to practice*: Make a vow to practice meditation by wishing that all sentient beings be blessed by the light of the Buddha, that they gain an enhanced wisdom, their roots of kindness be developed, and their worries be dissipated. At the same time, follow the practice of the Six Paramitas in order to establish a Pure Land on earth.

B. *Meditation*: While meditating, imagine the joyful light of compassion completely engulfing oneself. Meditate on one's parents, relatives, all BLIA members, one's country, and all sentient beings of all Dharma realms, so that together everyone will be able to attain Buddhahood in the Land of the Pure Lotus.

## 4. Actualization

This practice requires the three karmas of body, speech, and mind to harmonize with the mind of the Buddha. There are four levels of practice:

A. *Making vows*: Start every morning by making four vows to:

(1) Benefit all beings without limit.

(2) End all passions and delusions.

(3) Learn all methods needed to accomplish these vows.

(4) Become perfect in the Dharma, in order to be in harmony with the vows of the bodhisattvas.

These vows are to be carried out in the course of one's daily activities: eating, getting dressed, working, and interacting with family and others. Various vows of kindness can be made to cultivate one's mind under different circumstances. Remember that vows are the basis for the completion of compassionate deeds.

B.   *Pure practice*: Use wisdom and compassion to aid others in their endeavors. Lead them to the Dharma by supporting their cultivation of the Bodhi mind and take the Five Precepts, Bodhisattva Precepts, Eight Precepts, and even the Monastic Precepts. Always use the Noble Eightfold Path as a guiding light.

C.   *Repentance*: By repenting, one understands clearly one's own past negative and distructive actions. One's mind is able to mature only with the practice of repentance. Those who repent are able to see through the causes and conditions of their actions, and become aware of how they have been negative and distructive. Through repentance, one can learn from one's mistakes and failures. Therefore, it is said that repentance is the most meritorious of actions.

D.   *Transformation*: Planting seeds in the fields for the next harvest.

There are three types of transference:

> (1) Bodhi transformation – From cause to effect, from negative to positive, and from delusion to enlightenment.
>
> (2) People transformation – From self to others, from few to many, and from a lower level to a higher level.
>
> (3) Practical transformation – From phenomena to truth, from digression to completion, and from attachment to the Middle Path.

The practices described above embody all bodhi vows and cultivation, and are in harmony with the Buddha's mind. In practice, one can develop one's own Pure Land and, together with the effort of all sentient beings, we can build a Pure Land on earth.

I hope that all Buddha's Light members are diligent in their practice, bearing in mind that all sentient beings, in all Dharma realms, will together bring about a new epoch of joy and light for all mankind.

**Exercises:**

1. What constitutes the various methods and practices of Buddha's Light Samadhi?
2. Why do members of the BLIA use Buddha's Light Samadhi as daily practice?
3. Describe the four stages of practice of Buddha's Light Samadhi.

## Chapter 10
# The Main Points of BLIA Procedures and Conduct

"When one does not follow regulations, then one is not able to complete tasks." Since its inception, the BLIA has grown by reaching out to the world through its members working toward common goals. The BLIA has lofty goals, a rich spirit, and most importantly, has *unity*, which is expressed both through its ceremonies and conduct. For example, the lotus gesture, wearing of the BLIA vest, methods of practice, chanting of verses, guidelines that are used to hold its activities, meeting procedures, and the manner in which others are addressed, are all expressions of the BLIA's spirit of unity. Once you become a member of the BLIA, you are a member for life. Together we can work to build a brighter future.

The following will illustrate the main points of BLIA procedures.

### A. Guidelines for a meeting
1. BLIA members should attend a variety of meetings. When members attend an activity or gathering, they should be on time, or arrive early, if possible. The organizer of the meeting should also be on time.
2. BLIA members should wear their vests when attending meetings and activities. This encourages a team spirit.
3. At the beginning and end of every meeting, members should sing the Anthem of the Triple Gem to affirm the beliefs of BLIA members.
4. During a meeting, the president's speech should be concise and clear. Reports should last between three and five minutes. Either at the very beginning of a meeting or in the middle is the best time for guest speakers to present their information.

5. When a sub-chapter has a meeting, the president acts as chairperson. Seats should be provided for previous presidents, advisors, consultants, and VIPs.

6. When holding a meeting, the secretary should have a repre sentative record the minutes.

7. All resolutions passed during a BLIA meeting should not contradict the bylaws of local BLIA chapters and sub-chapters.

8. BLIA members should enthusiastically join all meetings. If members are unable to attend, they should let the organizers know. During the course of a year, each member should try to speak at least three times, rather than only listen.

**B. Specific rules of conduct**

1. Members should not borrow or lend money. If they operate a business together, they should have a formal contract. Their profit and loss should not have anything to do with the BLIA.

2. BLIA members should not use BLIA meetings to conduct non-BLIA business with each other.

3. Without the approval of headquarters, BLIA members should not receive private donations.

4. When BLIA members join together, it is best to have at least three people in a group.

5. If BLIA members are invited to join community or monastery activities, they should be assigned by their sub-chapter president. The BLIA vest should be worn.

6. When it is time to celebrate the Buddha's Birthday, the New Year, a member's birthday, or other special occasions, members can show their respect by mailing congratulatory cards issued by the BLIA.

7. When there is a marriage, a funeral, or an occasion for celebration, members can actively assist or join in the chanting. They should not take a donation.

8. Members of the BLIA can participate in weddings, funerals, celebrations, and chanting activities for each other. However, members should not perform Dharma functions or repentance cermonies.

9. The members of the BLIA should follow these seven principles of behavior:
   A. Do not borrow or lend money.
   B. Avoid improper conduct between men and women.
   C. Avoid negative thoughts and negative views.
   D. Avoid gossip.
   E. Do not start rumors or make trouble for others.
   F. Avoid involvement in Sangha business.
   G. Do not arrange a Dharma function by yourself.

10. If there is a conflict between BLIA members, they should resolve it by using the seven ways to resolve disputes.

## C. Social relationships

1. When members greet each other, they should make the lotus gesture, and when addressing each other they should say, "Upasaka," "Upasika," "Dharma brother," or "Dharma sister."

2. Each month, BLIA members should make at least three calls to other members to discuss the Dharma, and show concern by visiting each other.

3. The president should communicate with local monasteries and the headquarters if members of the BLIA are having weddings, funerals, or other celebrations, in order to invite monastics to chant and give blessings.

4. When members have weddings, funerals, or other celebrations, the sub-chapters can present flowers, memorial banners, or give donations to show their support.

## D. Items for practice

1. Members should constantly recite the BLIA Verse, for example, each day after morning and evening chanting, before meals, and especially at a gathering.

2. Each day, BLIA members should chant the *Heart Sutra* at least once in the morning or evening. They should take Buddha's Light Samadhi Practice as their daily practice.

3. BLIA members need to be diligent in their practice, and should make every effort to study Buddhism. Members may take the Sutra Pitaka as their basic Buddhist text, which they can read and study in order to increase their understanding. They should join at least one of the reading groups in the temple so they can delve deeper into the Buddha's teachings.

4. BLIA members should read Buddha's Light prayers every day, emphasize gratitude, and make vows to enhance their beliefs.

5. To propagate the spirit of humanistic Buddhism is the goal of the BLIA. Members should read books from the Fo Guang publishing house, in order to deepen their understanding of the ideas and spirit of humanistic Buddhism.

6. Each year, both the association and sub-chapters should celebrate the Day of Buddha's Light. They can hold many kinds of activities, such as fairs, seminars, talent shows, musical performances or concerts, outdoor mural painting, or sports competitions.

7. When visiting temples, members should go to the Buddha Hall and bow to the Buddha upon arrival and departure.

8. BLIA members should behave with mindfulness and not rush around. Always remember the Four Manners: walk like the wind, stand like a pine, sit like a bell, and lie down like a bow.

9. BLIA members should cultivate the Seven Characters: respect, tolerance, equality, joy, morality, forbearance (forgiveness), and humanism.

10. BLIA members should have the Seven Spiritual Properties: belief, enthusiasm, inspiration, joy, befriending all, compassion, and treasuring one's good fortune.

11. In their daily lives, BLIA members should practice and experience: joy and harmony, oneness and coexistence, respect and tolerance, equality and peace, wholeness and freedom, and nature and life.

12. BLIA members should cultivate the Seven Purifications:
    a. purification of name
    b. purification of objective
    c. purification of members
    d. purification of motivation
    e. purification of relationships
    f. purification of language
    g. purification of meeting

The aim of the main points of BLIA procedures and conduct is to provide members with guidelines for daily activities, self-cultivation, and relationships with other members. If everyone can follow these main points, it will facilitate activities and enhance individual practice, relationships, and experience.

**Exercises:**

1. What are the principles that BLIA members should observe when attending meetings?

2. What rules should BLIA members obey when conducting business?

3. What etiquette should BLIA members practice when interacting with one another?

4. How should BLIA members practice spiritual development in their daily lives?

# Chapter 11
# Knowing Humanistic Buddhism Through Fo Guang Shan

$F$o Guang Shan was established in 1967. Twenty-five years later, the BLIA was created. Both introduced a form of Chinese Buddhism that reaches out to the whole world. Fo Guang devotees base their practice of humanistic Buddhism on emulating the Buddhas and Bodhisattvas. We follow the examples set by Manjusri, Samantabhadra, Avalokiteshvara, and Ksitigarbha. Their vows and compassion support the spreading of Buddhism worldwide. As a result of more than thirty years of effort in promoting humanistic Buddhism, Fo Guang Shan has received recognition and respect throughout the world. The following four points illustrate the spirit of humanistic Buddhism.

1. **Promote respect and tolerance, and improve harmony in the world**

   Buddhism emphasizes respect and tolerance. Long ago, when anyone from the four castes joined the order, they were named Shi, making them all equal. Fo Guang Shan not only respects and tolerates the differences between individuals; we advocate harmony in all relationships. In an effort to create harmony among different traditions, we organized the Chinese-Tibetan Cultural Association, we held the Sutric-Tantric Buddhist Conference, and we offered the International Buddhist Sangha Seminar. We have also supported the World Buddhist Fellowship Association in holding its meetings in the United States and Australia. At the International Ordination Ceremony, which was held in India, men and women from twenty-six countries and many traditions, including the Theravada and Sutric-Tantric traditions, were represented.

Fo Guang Shan has established relationships with Dharma-kaya Temple in Thailand, and the Tongdosa and the Buddhist College in Songgwangsa, in Korea. In South Africa we estab-lished a Buddhist college in order to raise the living stan- dards of the local people. We have prepared disaster relief meals in the countries of Paraguay, Peru, Costa Rica, Papua New Guinea, and various Pacific islands. In Taiwan, we asked our aboriginal resi-dents neighbors to join the BLIA annual conference. We also donate to and sponsor Christian churches and hospitals.

Venerable Master Hsing Yun has met four times for dis-cussions with His Holiness the Dalai Lama, and had a dialogue with Pope John Paul II. Fo Guang Shan monastics have been in-vited to conduct a blessing before a government meeting in the United States; Master Hsing Yun has taken a group to Mainland China to teach the Dharma and visit his hometown. These activi-ties bring people hope and mutual respect, developing tolerance between different nations, cultures, and ethnic groups, while promoting world peace.

## 2. Focus on morality and ethics to encourage practice in eve-ryday life

To promote the purification of minds and to emphasize prac-tice in everyday life is the way to practice humanistic Buddhism. For many years we have held summer camps, seminars, short-term monastic retreats, eight precepts retreats, five precepts retreats, and bodhisattva retreats. Each Sunday, in all branch temples throughout the world, we hold Amitabha chanting. After the temporary closing to the public of Fo Guang Shan in 1997, devotees requested that we hold weekend retreat, providing them with an opportunity to practice and listen to the Dharma. Other ongoing activities like meditation sessions, pilgrimages, the copying of sutras, repentance ceremonies, study groups, music and artistic design classes, and community sharing are also held. We also hold large functions that are not regularly scheduled, such as, Return to the Era of the Buddha, Loving Compassion Program, Rediscover Your Mind, Seven Admonitions Program, and the triple practice of Chan, Pure Land, and Esoteric Buddhism. Through these activities we introduce Buddhism to our families and become a force for the purification of our society.

The humanistic Buddhism of Fo Guang Shan focuses on the family because we believe that by emphasizing Buddhist education we can pass our beliefs on to the next generation. To this end, Fo Guang Shan has established many kindergartens, orphanages, day care centers, and Chinese schools. We have established Pu Men High School, Hsi Lai University, and Fo Guang University.

We hope that through education we can purify people's minds, re-establish morality, and promote ethics. Humanistic Buddhism emphasizes living the teachings. Fo Guang Shan holds adulthood ceremonies, wedding ceremonies, Three Refuge ceremonies, and funeral services. Buddhist ceremonial rituals are another way we can reach the goal of Buddhism becoming a part of our lives.

### 3. Establishing institutions and Buddhist groups

Fo Guang Shan takes the well being of society as its model. We follow Buddhist teachings and emulate the expedient methods of Chan masters. The arrangement of the Buddha Hall and all Dharma functions follow tradition. The signals of the bell, the drum, and the boards, as well as the monastic rules, all follow traditional monastery practices.

In practice we stress teamwork, with the leader following tradition. If something does not conform to Buddhist standards of conduct we do not incorporate it into our practice. We rely exclusively on the Dharma. Through this kind of belief, we honor the past and pass our spirit on to future generations.

For more than thirty years we have established modern religious groups. We give equal opportunity to both monks and nuns. We emphasize the promotion of today's technology and education to assist in career development. For example, the *Buddha's Light Tripitaka* editing and revising committee re-edits using a modern form of punctuation, paragraph arrangement, commentary, and footnotes. Another example is the *Chinese Buddhist Sutra Treasury Collection*, which was published in modern vernacular to increase reader acceptance. With the assistance of the Education and Legal Assistance departments, Fo Guang Shan's publications are sent to schools and prisons.

*Universal Gate* and *Awaken the World* are Buddhist magazines written in a literary style that can be appreciated by everyone. Moreover, we have established over twenty libraries and nine art galleries, filled with rich examples of Buddhist literature and art, which add beauty to our lives.

To promote education, we have established sixteen Buddhist colleges, and four universities, offered world Buddhist exams, and organized international Buddhist conferences. Buddhist summer camps, Buddhist seminars, City Buddhist Colleges and Sunday schools promote the spreading of bodhi seeds throughout the world.

For lay people, we have created the system of Jiao Shi, and Shi Gu. The establishment of the BLIA has broadened the possibilities for devotees to participate, especially with the creation of the lay Dharma teacher program, thus lay people and monastics can share the responsibility of spreading the Dharma together. Fo Guang Shan is a Buddhist organization with a system of beliefs and great vows. Buddhism encourages people to come together. With the support of the Dharma, everyone can generate their *bodhicitta*, based on the bodhisattva spirit: " I will not worry about my own happiness, instead, I hope that all sentient beings can be free from suffering."

More than a hundred temples in Taiwan and abroad teach the Dharma to purify people's minds. A reporter from the *China Daily News*, Miss Wu Ling-chiao, after visiting and interviewing people at Fo Guang Shan said, "Fo Guang Shan is a bodhisattva monastery that teaches humanistic Buddhism. Those who focus only on their own awakening should not go to Fo Guang Shan." This is quite true.

### 4. Teaching humanistic Buddhism, establishing the Buddha's Light Pure Land

The Buddhism that the Buddha gave us is *humanistic* and humanistic Buddhism stresses the integration of our spiritual practice into all aspects of our daily lives. Humanistic Buddhism has six characteristics: humanism, emphasis on daily life, altruism, joyfulness, timeliness, and universality. Today, we follow Buddhism's spirit of focusing on the present moment, giving guidance and joy. We teach humanistic Buddhism and work to establish a Buddha's Light Pure Land.

Illustrating the importance of the Buddhist focus on life today, Fo Guang Shan established the Buddha's Light Retirement Home to provide seniors with a comfortable place to live. We have also established Da Tzu Orphanage to care for children who have no parents. We created the Buddha's Light Clinic and Yun Shui free medical service. We also set aside Wan Shou Cemetery was developed, so the processes of birth, life, old age, sickness, and death can all be attended to at Fo Guang Shan. We have benefactors meetings so that those people who have contributed to Buddhism in this lifetime do not have to wait until death to gain merits.

As part of our educational process, Fo Guang Shan focuses on publishing Buddhist books, holding Buddhist lectures, seminar, and discussion groups, and visiting families. We bring Buddhism to families so they can apply the practice in their daily lives. For many years we have spread the Dharma on the radio. We've established a television committee that is responsible for creating such programs as "Nectar," "The Gate of Faith," "Lecture on the Sixth Patriarch's Platform Sutra," "Hsing Yun's Chan Talk," and "Hsing Yun's Dharma Words." In 1997, responding to the needs of the time, the Buddha's Light Television Channel was founded. Using these different methods, we have spread the Dharma worldwide.

Fo Guang Shan promotes harmony in the human world. We encourage couples to respect and love one another. We not only focus on the education of parents and children, we also value the blissful life of the family. We promote the spirit of oneness and coexistence as we strive to introduce Buddhism to everyone.

Although the ultimate goal may be rebirth in the Western Pure Land or in the Medicine Buddha's Pure Land, once we purify our own minds the Pure Land exists at this very moment. In our professional capacities, we conduct business in the world based on a spirit of non-attachment. We light a bright lantern for the saha world. Buddha's Light Pure Land is a collection of all the Pure Lands of all the Buddhas. The achievement of humanistic Buddhism is this Buddha's Light Pure Land.

**Exercises:**
1.  What is the Buddha's Light Pure Land?
2.  Why do people call Fo Guang Shan a bodhisattva monastery?
3.  How does Fo Guang Shan promote humanistic Buddhism?

# Chapter 12
## Verses from Buddhist Sutras Relevant to Humanistic Buddhism

*T*his chapter contains nearly one hundred excellent verses, collected from Buddhist scriptures and publications, along with quotes from eminent monastics. These verses can serve as a guideline for humanistic Buddhism, and furnish proof of its lineage.

### 1. Life and Environmental Protection

*If people cultivate and acquire various merits, but do not abolish killing, they gain no merit. Why? Because in future lives, they might be reborn with wealth, status, and significance, but they won't live long enough to enjoy them. In this case, one cannot benefit from wealth and status. Thus, of all the erroneous acts, killing is the most grievous one, and not killing is the supreme virtue.*
> *~ Treatise on the Perfection of Great Wisdom*

*The Buddha said: If a man born in this world is compassionate and does not kill, he can gain five states of joy. What are these five states? First, he gains longevity. Second, he is safe and serene. Third, wars, wild animals, or catastrophe will not harm him. Fourth, in the future he will be reborn in heavenly realms to enjoy infinite life. Fifth, in his next rebirth in this world, he will live a long life.*
> *~ Sutra on the Difference Between Good and Bad*

*Compassion is the father,*
*Bodhi mind the mother,*
*Good methods are like friends,*
*for they save all sentient beings.*
> *~ Sutra on the Collection of Correct Dharma*

*All beings fear death, and they all fear the pain of a club.*
*Think: how would this make you feel?*
*Then do not kill, and do not beat. Live peacefully with all*
*beings and do not add to the violence of this world.*
*Harm no one here, and you will pass your next life in peace.*

*~ Dharmapada*

*Due to one's orchard cultivation,the shade of trees is*
*pleasant and soothing.If one builds bridges and ships*
*to facilitate transportation,erects houses to shelter people,*
*digs wells to help quench people's thirst,or provides*
*rooms to accommodate travelers,his merits will surely*
*accumulate with time.If he also upholds the precepts strictly,*
*he will be reborn in heaven.*

*~ Samyukta Agama*

*The Buddha told the king of heaven:*
*There are seven methods, named "fields of merits."*
*Those who carry them out can go to heaven.*
*What are these seven methods?*
*First, building Buddhist temples and stupas.*
*Second, constructing bathing facilities, and planting orchards*
*and trees.*
*Third, providing medicines and aid to cure and protect suf-*
*ferers.*
*Fourth, manufacturing sturdy ships to facilitate transporta-*
*tion.*
*Fifth, building bridges to transport the weak.*
*Sixth, digging wells near main roads to accommodate trav-*
*elers.*
*Seventh, building toilets to serve the public.*
*These are the seven things that can elevate people to heaven.*

*~ Sutra on Virtues and Merits*

*As Buddhists set captive animals free with kindness and*
*compassion, they should keep the following in mind:*
*All men are our fathers,*
*All women are our mothers.*
*For many lifetimes we have been born as their offspring.*
*All beings in the six realms are thus our parents.*
*Killing them and eating their flesh is like killing our own*
*parents, or killing ourselves.*

*~ Brahmajala Sutra*

*People who are good at seeking self-protection,*
*guard their own lives.*
*Self-protection with equality,*
*means protecting all life forms equally.*

*~ Samyukta Agama*

*When we protect ourselves, we also protect others.*
*When others protect themselves, they also protect us.*
*Associate with good friends intimately, emulate and learn*
*from them, and be mindful of cultivation and experiences.*
*This is called protecting oneself and protecting others.*
*What does it mean to protect oneself and others? It simply*
*means do not terrify others, do not violate others, do not harm*
*others. In addition, we sympathize with others kindly.*
*This is protecting others and oneself. Self-protectors cultivate*
*the four mindfullnesses, and so do the protectors of others.*

*~ Samyukta Agama*

*Constantly harbor humility in mind,*
*and sympathize with all beings.*
*Often keep thoughts of protecting all beings,*
*including insects in the lower realm.*

*~ Dirgha Agama*

## 2.  Management and Education

*A king has five responsibilities toward his citizens.*
*What are they?*
*First, he rules all citizens without abusing authority, and without corruption.*
*Second, he recruits soldiers to defend the kingdom, and provides them with ample and timely provisions.*
*Third, he cultivates his actions and mind, to accumulate merit, ensuring infinite joy.*
*Fourth, he has faith in the advice given by the devoted and the loyal, but distrusts flattery. Thus, he harms no one.*
*Fifth, he takes worldly pleasures moderately, without over indulgence.*
*By fulfilling these five responsibilities, he will become famous, wealthy, and acquire great happiness. But if he is unable to fulfill these five responsibilities, a king will discover that all the rules in his kingdom will fail, that difficulties and chaos will arise, and that his soldiers will labor to exhaustion and, will be in low-spirits.*

*~ Dharmapada Parable Sutra*

*If one desires to defeat evil beings,*
*first of all, one needs to be kind hearted.*
*Then, one should examine and study the situation wisely.*
*Lastly, one should contemplate and think through the five bases before taking any action.*
*What are the five bases?*
*First, find out the truth and use it as a guideline.*
*Second, have a good sense of timing.*
*Third, do what is pertinent.*
*Fourth, use soft language, devoid of rudeness or filth.*
*Fifth, practice compassion and have no anger.*

*~ Bodhisattva-gocaropaya-visayavikurvana-nirdesa*

*A great householder upholds the following five rules*
*when associating with servants and maids.*
*First, provide meals and clothing in a timely manner.*
*Second, send for physicians in times of illness.*
*Third, does not punish or reproach them without good reason.*
*Fourth, do not steal their personal belongings.*
*Fifth, provide fair, equal treatment to all without partiality.*
*~ Sigalovada Sutra*

*There are five rules when servants and maids attend to their*
*masters:*
*First, rise early in the morning.*
*Second, do one's work attentively.*
*Third, take good care of your master's goods,*
*and do not give them away without permission.*
*Fourth, attend to the comings and goings of the master.*
*Fifth, praise the master, make no complaints or gossip.*
*~ Sigalovada Sutra*

*There are five things that a teacher should teach his students:*
*First, teach the student what you know.*
*Second, impart more knowledge and skills to your students,*
*than they can receive from other teachers.*
*Third, make sure your students remember what they have*
*learned.*
*Fourth, answer questions or problems that your students may*
*have.*
*Fifth, encourage and support your students in becoming wiser*
*than yourself.*
*~ Sigalovada Sutra*

*Support the student in learning;*
*ensure that the student has the ability to teach;*
*give the student skills of decernment;*

*guide the student into kindness;*
*and advise students to associate with good people.*
*These are the five responsibilities of a teacher.*

*~ Sigalovada Sutra*

*A student has five responsibilities towards his teacher.*
*First, show gratitude to your teacher.*
*Second, remember the goodness and mercy of your teacher.*
*Third, listen attentively to what is taught.*
*Fourth, remember your teacher dearly.*
*Fifth, honor your teacher publicly.*

*~ Sigalovada Sutra*

*Accomplished in his path, a student realizes the mercy of his teacher. He attends to his teacher when present.*
*He remembers and thinks of the teachings constantly, as a child thinking of his parents when they are absent.*

*~ Sutra of the Faithful Mind*

*Do not discard utensils containers that are coarse or badly made, for they can be used for storage.*
*Do not discard people who are foolish or cheap,*
*for they can be useful in something.*

*~ Commentary on Fo Shuo Pei Sutra*

*Everything takes time.*
*If the time is not ripe,*
*one who tries to force things to happen,*
*will gain nothing but pains and sorrows.*
*Thus, we ought to discern good timing and bad.*

*~ Sutra of One Hundred Parables*

*One has to eliminate one's own faults,before*
*teaching others.For it is not logical for one*

*who is in error,to teach others to do righ thing.*
*Thus, bodhisattvas have to give, uphold precepts,*
*be content and be diligent, prior to teaching others to do so.*
*~ Sutra on the Upasaka Precepts*

*Rely on the Dharma, not on the person.*
*Rely on wisdom, not on knowledge.*
*Rely on the true meaning, not on words.*
*Rely on definitive teachings, not on interpretive teachings.*
*~ Mahaparinirvana Sutra*

*Strategies should be far-reaching,*
*while decisions must be personal.*
*When strategies are numerous, one can ponder over the dis-*
*advantages and the benefits in numerous situations.*
*By making one's own decision, one can assess whats right and*
*wrong in the monastery.*
*~ Precious Teaching of the Chan Monastery*

*The silent are not necessarily foolish;*
*The eloquent are not necessarily wise;*
*The plain and shabby are not necessarily rebellious;*
*The obedient are not necessarily loyal.*
*Thus, a wise person doesn't rely solely on words, and he does*
*not have hidden motives when choosing students.*
*~ Precious Teaching of the Chan Monastery*

*A good monastic leader gives more weight to the feelings of*
*the public than to his own.*
*He gives more consideration to what the public sees and*
*hears than to what he does.*
*Thus, he understands what the public will accept, and also*
*knows where the public places their hearts.*
*~ Precious Teaching of the Chan Monastery*

*Taking refuge in one's own inner Sangha,one wishes that all beings can lead the public and manage their affairs without any hindrances.*

*~ Flower Garland Sutra*

*One who does not hold on to one's wealth,*
*does not differentiate whom he likes or despises,*
*and does not discern good times and bad,*
*this is the person who can manage the public.*

*~ Sutra on the Upasaka Precepts*

### 3. Family Ethics

A. *During one's lifetime, even if one lifts both parents on his shoulders, handsomely accommodates them, and generously provides for them with treasures, one cannot repay an iota of one's parents' kindness.*

*~ Five-Part Vinaya*

B. *While providing for one's parents and the elderly of one's family, one ought to be amiable, gentle, speak with humility, and be devoid of coarseness or duplicity. One also needs to cultivate generosity and speak the truth.*

*~ Samyukta Agama*

C. *Support one's parents with kindness, then your family life will be joyous and peaceful. For a father's grace is as high as a mountain, and that of a mother is as deep as the ocean.*

*~ Contemplations on the Basis of Mind Sutra*

D. *If one pays filial respect to one's parents at home, this is superior to the field of happiness. If one spreads the idea of filial piety in this lifetime, he will acquire unlimited joy and merits in future lifetimes.*

*~ Dharma Verses of Nagarjuna*

E. *A son should support his parents in the following five ways:*
   *First, by augmenting their wealth;*
   *Second, by managing their business affairs;*
   *Third, by satisfying their needs;*
   *Fourth, by not going against their will;*
   *Fifth, by offering to them all of his personal belongings.*
   ~ *Sigalovada Sutra*

F. *Parents should give the following five things to their children:*
   *First, teach them to eliminate vice and cultivate virtue.*
   *Second, teach them living skills, as well as reading and writing.*
   *Third, teach them rules and precepts.*
   *Fourth, allow them to be married when they want.*
   *Fifth, give them what the family owns.*
   ~ *Sigalovada Sutra*

G. *A husband ought to look after his wife in the folowing five*
   *ways:*
   *First, always respect her.*
   *Second, provide her with food and clothing in a timely*
   *fasion.*
   *Third, give her jewelry.*
   *Fourth, turn over the family finance to her.*
   *Fifth, do not keep mistresses or gamble.*
   ~ *Sigalovada Sutra*

H. *A wife should attend to her husband in the following five*
   *ways:*
   *First, when the husband returns from outside, she ought to*
   *rise and greet him.*
   *Second, during his absence, she should do housekeeping,*
   *cooking, and wait for him.*
   *Third, do not engage in a love affair with another man and*
   *do not talk back to the husband.*
   *Fourth, take the husband's advice and suggestions, and do*

*not hide goods from him.*
*Fifth, only rest when the husband does so.*

~Sigalovada Sutra

I. *A woman should not be proud of her gook looks. For good*
*looks is not true beauty. Only a beautiful disposition that is*
*admired and respected by everyone is called beauty.*

~ Sutra of Lady Yu Ye

J. *A woman has five good thingsto attend to for her in-laws*
*and husband:*
*First, rest late and rise early to manage housekeeping, and*
*serve relish to her in-laws and husband before herself*
*Second, look after family goods.*
*Third, watch her own language. Be tolerant, not angry.*
*Fourth, be as dignified and cautious as possible.*
*Fifth, serve her in-laws and husband respectfully and*
*single-mindedly. Make them reputable and admired by*
*people, and make all relatives happy.*

~Sutra of Lady Yu Ye

K. *A person should do five things regarding his relatives*
*First, he should be generous to them.*
*Second, he should speak to them with good and true words.*
*Third, he should do beneficial deeds for them.*
*Fourth, he should share one's profits with them.*
*Fifth, he should not cheat them.*

~ Dirgha Agama

## 4. Abolishing destructive and Cultivating Virtues

*When destructive thoughts and feelings spring into your*
*mind, it hurts you. This can be likened to rust on iron, that*
*eventually eats it away.*

~ Commentary on Fo Shuo Pei Sutra

*These are the five highest ways that a person should minister to ascetics and Brahmins: By being kind in deed, kind in speech, kind in thought, by keeping one's home open to them, and by supplying for their bodily needs. These are the six highest ways for ascetics and Brahmins, thus ministered to by him to reciprocate: By restraining him from destructive- ness, by encouraging him to do good, by being benevolently compassionate towards him, by teaching him what has not been heard, and by showing him the way to heaven.*

*~ Dirgha Agama*

*There are four ways to restrain from evil for one who is well-born and of high birth: By restricting him from doing evil deeds, by pointing out the way of integrity, by showing him benevolent compassion, and by showing him the way to heaven. This is the way to be at peace and free from fear.*

*~Dirgha Agama*

*Non-provocation will stop a fight before it can begin; A compassionate person sympathizes with all sentient beings; Since no sentient beings are harmed, he is praised by all Buddhas.*

*~ Ekottaragama*

*One would rather die of poverty and hunger in order not to break the precepts than live in the material world without guarding the Dharma path.*

*~ Sutra on the Six Paramitas*

*Greedy people like to accumulate material wealth without ever being satisfied. They are confused by the ignorance and hatred springing from their polluted minds, which leads them to suffering. Those who are wise should contemplate fulfillment.*

~ *Bodhisattva-gocaropaya-visayavikurvana-nirdesa*

*You should know that an angry mind is worse than a fierce fire. Always be on guard and watch yourselves so as not let this mind obtain entry. No brigand can steal your merit and virtue more surely than anger and rage.*

~ *Sutra of Buddha's BequeathedTeaching*

*Anyone who wants to acquire wealth must know that there are six ways of gaining wealth, which run contrary to Buddhist morality. These six ways are:*

1. *devious or tricky ways*
2. *ill-timed ways*
3. *careless ways or ways which use alcoholic beverages*
4. *ways which depend on evil companions*
5. *ways which depend on prostitution*
6. *lazy or slothful ways*

~ *Sigalovada Sutra*

*Upon seeing that someone's knowledge is greater than yours, do not give way to jealousy. When your knowledge is greater than that of others, do not give way to pride.*

~ *Sutra on the Upasaka Precepts*

*A face without anger is a type of offering;*
*Speech without anger generates wonderful fragrances;*
*A heart without anger is like a priceless gem;*
*the eternal truth is beyond worldly discrimination.*

~ *Sutra on Boy Kunti*

*There are two types of upright speech:*
*Following the Dharma will help the listener believe, understand, and realize the truth.*
*Following reason will help the listener be free from doubt.*

*There are two types of gentle speech:*
*With comforting words, the listener will be secure and will*
*learn from you.*
*With tender words, the listener will feel joy and will be willing*
to *accept what you teach*

.

*There are two types of harmonious speech:*
*To foster harmonious relationships, if people are arguing, try*
*to persuade them to stop. Show no pride, be humble, and re-*
*spect people.*
*To foster a harmonious practice, inspire other practitioners to*
*keep up their practice. Help them to overcome the obstacles*
*on their path, and knowing how to discriminate between and*
*harmonize Bodhi and defilements.*

*There are two types of truthful speech:*
*Tell the truth. When you have something, say you have*
*something.*
*When you don't have something, say you don't have some-*
*thing;*
*When something is right, say it is right;*
*When something is wrong, say it is wrong.*
*Tell the ultimate truth: All sentient beings possess Buddha*
*Nature; the Tathagata's Nirvana is eternal.*
                    *~ Tang, Master Yong Jia Xuan Jue(665-713)*

*Do not gossip about the good points and bad points of*
*other. In the end, one will suffer for one's wrong speech. Re-*
*fraining from talk and thus not creating verbal karma, is the*
*best way to cultivate.*
                            *~ Song, Zu Shou Huai Shen*

*When one accomplishes these four things, the Buddha will*

*be present at the passing moment of this person: Whenever
someone needs things, he provides he holds a deep belief and
understanding of the Dharma he makes generous offerings to
the bodhisattvas He diligently makes offerings to the Triple
Gem.*

*~ Sutra on the Girl Miao Hui*

## 5. Managing Wealth

*When you begin in a trade or profession,
it is appropriate to accumulate wealth.
Once you have accumulated a measure of wealth,
you should divide it into four parts:
one part to be used for daily necessities,
two parts to be used for your profession,
one part to be saved in case of unexpected need.*

*~ Samyukta Agama*

*All wealth can be divided into four parts:
One part should be deposited as savings to earn interest as
reserve for the unexpected needs of the family.
One part should be used to support the daily needs of the
family.
One part should be used as charity contributions for the
people whose parents and spouses have passed away in order
to allow them to cultivate a measure of happiness.
One part should be used to assist friends and relatives who
travel a long distance from their hometown.*

*~ Contemplations on the Basis of Mind Sutra*

*There are three ways to distribute the wealth of a government:
The first portion should be offered to the Buddhas and Bhik-
shus.
The second portion should be given to those who have suf-
fered from poverty and to those whose parents have passed*

*away.*
*The third portion should be reserved for the purpose of managing -of the government.*

> ~ *Maharatnakuta*

*These are four best ways to use one's wealth:*
*The first way is to support one's parents and spouse.*
*The second way is to look after one's workers and guests.*
*The third way is to serve the needs of one's friends and relatives.*
*The forth way is to give to one's government, to shramanas (monks), and hermits.*

> ~ *Parinirvanasutra*

*One who is not satisfied, even though he is rich, is poor.*
*One who is satisfied, even though he is poor, is rich.*

> ~ *Sutra of Buddha's Bequeathed Teaching*

*Accumulation of wealth starts from a small amount of treasure, such as bees collecting honey from the flowers. Eventually the wealth will increase daily, providing that the treasure is not being wasted.*

> ~ *Sigalovada Sutra*

*Although we may become a billionaire, the desires of our mind should not be unleashed. In contrast, we should make more charitable contributions without any feelings of arrogance.*

> ~ *Sutra on Upasaka Precepts*

## 6. Friendship Skills

*Generosity, praise, good behavior, and fellowship—these four methods will bring harmony to the entire world.*

> ~ *Abhidharma Samgiti Paryayapada*

*If you handle the grass that a fish has been laid on, your hand will smell like a fish. This is what it is like to associate with destructive friends.*

~ *Abhiniskramana Sutra*

*When we live with a good person, before long we stop noticing how he changes us for the better. It is as if we have moved into a room full of orchids; before long we stop noticing their fragrance.*

~ *Abhiniskramana Sutra*

*Do not associate with destructive friends and do not do foolish things. Befriend good people who are the superior among all people. By associating with destructive friends, you will plant destructive seeds and will live long in the dark, even if you have a good nature.*

~ *Ekottaragama*

*Do not slander others, and do not differentiate between right and wrong. Yet, be mindful if your own behavior is correct or not.*

~ *Ekottaragama*

*As human beings, we should delight in moral people and be fond of good people without jealousy.*

~ *Sutra on Ananda's Questions Concerning the Auspicious and Inasupicious*

*We can see that a friend is eloquent but devious by the following: if he exposes the faults of others, while concealing his own, and praises others to their faces, while blaming them behind their backs.*

~ *Sigalovada Sutra*

*One should treat friends and relatives by the following five rules: First, seeing they are doing destructive things, one should stop, warn, and coax them in private. Second, one should rush to protect them when they need support. Third, one should not disclose what they told him in confidence. Fourth, one should show them respect and admiration. Fifth, one should aid them materially.*

*~ Sigalovada Sutra*

*There are four kinds of destructive or negative friends: first, there are those who harbor hatred in their minds while pretending to be true friends. second, there are those who say nice words in front of people but harsh words behind their back. third, there are those who, when friends are facing hardship, show concern to their face, but are delighted and happy behind their back. fourth, there are those who may act as intimate, dear relatives or friends, but who actually harbor hatred and deviousness in their hearts.*

*~ Sigalovada Sutra*

*There are four kinds of true friends: first are those who, seeing friends in poverty, try to assist them in them making a living. Second are those who do not argue, fight, or judge with friends. Third are those who keep in touch with friends frequently. Fourth are those whose friends are constantly kept in mind.*

*~ Sigalovada Sutra*

*A true friend possesses four characteristics: First, he prevents friends from engaging in conflicts and fighting with others. Second, he persuades friends not to associate with negative people. Third, he encourages friends into making a living when they are not doing so. Fourth, he guides friends into taking a liking to Buddhist sutras and Buddhist ways.*

*~ Sigalovada Sutra*

*A false friend possesses four characteristics: First, he gets furious even when slightly offended. Second, when asked to aid in urgent matters, he will refuse. Third, when he learns that some friend has an emergency, he will hide away. Fourth, when he sees that someone is dying, he discards them as if not knowing. The Buddha said that we should choose good people as our friends, and stay away from bad ones. Associating with true friends, I shall attain Buddhahood.*

*~ Sigalovada Sutra*

*There are four kinds of friends, this you must know. One is like a flower, another like a scale. One like a mountain, and one like the earth. What does it mean "like a flower"? In good times they place us on their head. If we wither, they throw us away. If we are doing well, they treat us well. If we become poor, they abandon us. What does it mean "like a scale"? When we are heavy with a burden, they tip their heads. When our burden is light, they raise their heads. When we have possessions, they respect us. When we have nothing, they become haughty and proud. What does it mean "like a mountain"? Birds and beasts flock there as if to a golden mountain; their fur and feathers reflect its light. Greatness gives greatness to others and shares their joys and blessings. What does it mean "like the earth"? Great good fortune and great wealth cause all to offer their respects. If the wealthy one is generous and helpful, all will be grateful as well.*

*~ Commentary on Fo Shuo Pei Sutra*

*There are three important ways to associate with true friends. First, when friends are on a mistaken path, we should point this out and ask them to correct their course. Second, when friends prosper, we should be filled with joy. Third, when friends suffer a mishap, we should not abandon them.*

*~ Sutra on Past and Present Causes and Effects*

*If one abolishes killing, and also persuades others to do so; if one is practicing the right view, and also teaches others to do so; then that person can be called a true friend.*

*~ Mahaparinirvana Sutra*

*There are four ways in which bodhisattvas are accomplished and cause people to believe what they say. What are these four ways? First, if they say they must cultivate themselves, this ensures that they do so. Second, they do not conceal any deficiencies or faults in front of theirtrue friends. Third, they do not criticize the Dharma that they have learned. Fourth, they ds not harbor any negative thought against any of their teachers.*

*~ Sutra on the Girl Miao Hui*

## 7. Ways to Nurture Our Health

*If one overeats, he will be idle because of his excessive weight. In this lifetime and in future lifetimes, he will have many problems with health, sleep, and in dealings with other people. He will be constantly sleepy and will easily become confused and bored. Therefore, one ought to be moderate in eating.*

*~ Bodhisattva-gocaropaya-visayavikurvana-nirdesa*

*Overeating creates five difficulties: First, one sleeps more than needed. Second, one sickens easily. Third, one is filled with lofty lusts. Fourth, one cannot chant or read sutras. Fifth, one clings to this world.*

*~ The Buddha's Medicine Sutra*

*One should treat meals just as if one is taking medication. Don't take a strong liking on to palatable dishes or a dislike to unsavory food. One should take one's meals to maintain a healthy body and be free of hunger and thirst.*

*~ Sutra of The Buddha's Bequeathed Teachings*

*Under the following conditions people become ill: First, by sitting for a long time without eating anything. Second, by eating without self-control, Third, because of worries and anxiety, Fourth, due to exhaustion, Fifth, through excessive sensuality, Sixth, through anger, Seventh, by not moving one's bowels, Eighth, by not urinating, Ninth, by suppressing burping, and Tenth, by not relieving one's flatulence.*

~ *The Buddha's Medicine Sutra*

*There are five benefits to be gained by walking. What are they? First, one develops a capability for walking. Second, one increases one's physical strength. Third, one will require less sleep. Fourth, one can digest food without creating health problems in one's digestive organs. Fifth, walkers more easily focus their minds for longer periods of time.*

~ *Sutra on the Three Contemplations on the Location of Mind*

*To have no illness is the greatest blessing. To be satisfied with what you have is the greatest fortune. True friends are the best of all relatives. Nirvana is the supreme peace.*

~ *Magnificent Life of the Prince Sutra*

*One should be mindful on eating in moderation, for one's digestive organs should not have to work overtime to absorb all the nutrients needed to keep one healthy and provide a long life.*

~ *Samyukta Agama*

*Reflecting on one's merit, contemplate from whence this meal comes. Assessing one's virtue, are we deserving of this offering? Guard the mind from various faults, greed in particular. Giving us strength, realize a meal is likened to medicine. In order to cultivate the Dharma path, we receive this meal.*

~ *Rules of the Chan Monastery*

*Walking meditation has five benefits: the development of the capability of walking for long periods of time, the improvement one's thinking, a decreased likelihood of illness, a better digestion of food and an increased ability to concentrate for long periods of time.*

*~ Four Part Vinaya*

*People who like to drink alcohol and engage in excessive conviviality should know that there are six disadvantages: First, the loss of money; Second, the creation of health problems; Third, engaging in conflicts and arguments; Fourth, disclosing personal privacy; Fifth, the inability to make judicious choices and looking after oneself; Sixth, a loss of wisdom and a gain in foolishness.*

*~ Sigalovada Sutra*

## 8. Secular Life

*Witnessing the ruin of segregation renders people co-operative. Spread the virtues of others and conceal their limitations. Do not say a word about things about which others are ashamed.*

*~ Sutra on the Upasaka Precepts*

*The compassionate are images of Guan-Yin, the magnanimous Mahasthamaprapta, the pure Shakyamuni, and the unaffected Amitabha.*

*~ Platform Sutra of the Sixth Patriarch*

*If one's mind is balanced, he does not need to observe the precepts. If one's behavior is upright, he does not need to meditate. If one thinks of the mercy of his parents, he would pay filial piety to them. If one knows relevence, he would have sympathy with his superiors and subordinates. If one knows*

*submission, he would create harmonious surroundings. If one*
*learns tolerance, he would eliminate vices.*

*~ Platform Sutra of the Sixth Patriarch*


*Good medication often tastes bad, sincere advice irritates*
*some people. If one reforms, he would gain wisdom. On the*
*contrary, if one conceals one's faults, he is unwise.*

*~ Platform Sutra of the Sixth Patriarch*


*If one has a good heart and is fortunate; he will be rich and*
*powerful untill old age and death. If one is fortunate but has an*
*evil heart, his good fortune will turn into mishaps. If one has a*
*good heart but bad fortune, his misfortunes will turn into good*
*fortune. If one has neither forture nor a good heart, he will be*
*poor, die young, and constantly run into troubles.*

*~ Tang, Master Huineng*

# Chapter 13
## Buddha's Light Organizational System

*I*nitially, when the Buddha developed the Sangha community, he took the Six Harmonies as guidelines for the organizational structure. What are the Six Harmonies?

1. Harmony of precepts.

    This is the equality of rules that everyone observes. The Buddha advocated taking the precepts as our teacher. It did not matter to what caste a person belonged, because all are regulated by the precepts and self-discipline.

2. Harmony of view.

    This means that everyone shares the same understanding and there is unity of thought. We take the Three Dharma Seals, the Four Noble Truths, and the Noble Eightfold Path of the Buddha's teaching as the foundation for our practice. By following these practices, a group can be of one mind.

3. Harmony of benefit.

    This refers to everyone sharing equally. Here there is balance in every economic aspect. Whatever is received from alms rounds, whether through the four kinds of offerings or from donors, all members of the Sangha share equally.

4. Harmony of association.

    This is the way to live together. The Sangha focuses on the spirit of teamwork. A monastic is not supposed to leave the Sangha and live alone. If a monastic wants to be alone, he or she must at least have some years of practice, as approved by the Buddha, before they can leave. An important principle of the Sangha that lives and practices together is to not disturb others.

5. Harmony of speech.

    This is the harmony of language. Using praise, encouragement, and loving words to inspire each other's practice can reduce conflict and argument.

6. Harmony of mind.

This makes everyone feel joyful, due to the equality that exists within the Sangha system, the unity of thought, economic fair treatment, the peace and joy of living together, and the harmony of language. The Sangha community can live together in harmony, sharing in the joy of the Dharma.

The Buddha took these Six Harmonies as guidelines for the Buddhist community, and the precepts to maintain a peaceful and pure community. Lay followers, who take refuge in the Triple Gem, Five Precepts, Eight Precepts, and the Bodhisattva Precepts, can system- atically improve their morality and purify their bodies and minds. Monastics, shramanera, and shramanerika who take the Ten Precepts, and bhiksu and bhiksuni, who take the full Precepts, use the same principles as guides for their bodies and minds in educational training.

Centuries after the Buddha entered parinirvana, Buddhism was introduced to China. The Chinese patriarchs and great masters followed the Buddha's spirit of precepts. They established monasteries and set rules, defined roles for monks and nuns, and divided monastic duties into forty-eight categories. These rules were used to unify the community and create harmony within the Sangha. The patriarchs and great masters, using these regulations as a guide, led Chan monasteries in developing rapidly. Their efforts led to Chan becoming a mainstream Buddhist school.

Since the inception of Fo Guang Shan in 1967, its organizational system has followed the Buddha's teachings. We follow the Six Harmonies, the precepts, and the rules of the monastery. We've established bylaws for the organization, trusting that the teachings of the Buddha can exist forever, that the sangha community can live harmoniously, and that the organization can develop without impediments. Here are some examples of Fo Guang Shan's system:

**1. The Personnel system.**
We evaluate personnel on various levels. The standard evaluation is based on the three principles of education, practice, and achievement. Monastic personnel are divided into five levels and nineteen grades. The five levels are Qing Qingshi, Xueshi, Xiushi, Kaishi and Da Shi.

Within the personnel system are five promotional stages, depending on the level. Through the Handing Down the Light Committee, the evaluation process is open and objective. At their first evaluation, each monastic may submit his or her own self-evaluation sheet, which may result in their receiving a higher evaluation. The evaluation meeting, which is held by the Religious Affairs Committee, invites related monastics to express their opinions. Anyone who feels unfairly treated can express his or her concerns to the Handing Down the Light Committee.

Those who follow the path of a layperson are called Qiaoshi and Shigu. The highest level of lay follower is Xiushi. Devotees must be careful not to be involved in monastic business. There are four levels of lay people: devotees, members, Dharma protectors, and benefactors. We choose the senior and respected devotees to lead. Those having a broad knowledge of Buddhism, clear speech, and right under-standing are invited to be our lay Dharma teachers, lay Dharma lecturers, and assistants, spreading the Dharma throughout the world.

**2. Assignment of duties**
The assignment of duties is based upon the premise that

each monastic's talent and individual potential should be developed to the highest degree. The assignment of duties and standards are as follows.

A. Those who are clear in speech and are quick thinking, are assigned cultural and educational duties. Examples of such duties are professor, lecturer, teacher, editor, or writer.

B. Those who are compassionate, kind, and friendly, will be assigned to attend to guests, sick members, and to provide medical care. They can also be employed in rest homes, orphanages, and do various kinds of charity work.

C. Those who are diligent, patient, and have organi- zational abilities can be assigned to such duties as abbot/abbess, vice-abbot, vice-abbess, supervisor, secretary, or administrative assistant.

D. Those who are aware of and understand financial matters, can accept duties in accounting and business.

E. Those who practice well and can set a good example may be assigned the position of leading venerable, master of ceremonies, chanting affairs, or managing a temple.

Beginners are assigned general duties in areas such as general affairs, gardening, serving meals, cooking, taking care of the oil lamps, and caring for the needs of guests. These duties can provide training as well as increase one's merit and wisdom.

All duties are evaluated on experience and ability based on the above five points. This system gives everyone an opportunity to learn all of the duties in a temple. A monastic's assignment can run from one to three years. In case of special needs, those who have three-year duties can receive an extension. At the end of six years, each monastic must accept the reassignment of the Religious Affairs Committee.

### 3. Financial system

Those who take care of money cannot make decisions regarding how it is spent. Those who manage financial duties are at the level of Xueshi. A separation must be maintained between those who make decisions and those who handle money.

### 4. Sharing benefits

All members of Fo Guang Shan have the opportunity to take a vacation, travel, study abroad, learn, and enjoy advanced practice. There are specific methods of handling travel to a foreign country, receiving medical care, and gaining old age benefits. There are other methods of handling parent's birthdays and the passing away of parents and other family members.

The Fo Guang Shan order has established its own rules. For example, we are not allowed to, build our own monastery, receive personal disciples or have private devotees, accept donations for oneself, accept personal favors from devotees, loan or borrow money, have personal savings, keep personal property (land or housing), or have personally prepared meals.

These rules foster an orderly environment that is free of disagreements. In this way, harmony within the Sangha can be passed on from generation to generation.

The organizational system of Fo Guang Shan follows the tradition of the great masters of the past. The highest attribute of the monastic system is teamwork. The two assemblies (male and female) follow the rules within this order. We espouse the belief that the monastery is number one, sentient beings are number one, devotees are number one, and Buddhism is number one. Our common guiding principle is that honor belongs to the Buddha, achievements belong to the majority, benefits belong to the monastery, and merits belong to the donors. In this way we deepen our lives, from imperfection to perfection. In the Fo Guang Shan order we encourage individual growth. Time will give us a good career, history will give us a fair evaluation, and belief will create eternal value.

**Exercises:**

1. How can we put the Six Harmonies into practice in our daily life?
2. How many departments are in the Fo Guang Shan Order? Please describe each.
3. How many cultural divisions are at Fo Guang Shan?
4. How many educational divisions are there?
5. How many charity divisions are there?
6. Describe the personnel system and its good points.
7. What is your opinion of the Fo Guang Shan rules?
8. Describe the characteristics of Fo Guang Shan monastics and the BLIA members.

# Chapter 14
# Guidelines for Buddha's Light Members

*C*ulture and Education are the foundations of Fo Guang Shan. The Buddha's original teachings stressed the importance of culture and education. He also emphasized the practice of loving kindness, joy, and equanimity. To continue in the spirit of Buddha's Light, the following working principles and ideals are what Buddha's Light members should follow and understand.

1. **The working principles of Buddha's Light members are to give others confidence, give others joy, give others hope, and render service to others.**

   Giving is the focus of the Four Guiding Principles. Whether you follow the Four Guiding Principles or the Six Paramitas, generosity is the number one practice. Giving comes from one's boundless inner treasure and resources.

   To give others confidence, each person needs to develop their own boundless confidence. Only then can one become a resource to benefit, teach, and save other sentient beings. We should be an inspiration to others, bolstering their determination and courage to go forward.

   To give others joy, we must first understand the endless joy that we possess within ourselves and then we can give to others. All Buddhas are enlightened because of joy. All great bodhisattvas save sentient beings in order to bring them joy. The Dharma and political leaders benefit others for the same reason. A family, because of its relationship with joy, will create a future of tolerance. With joy, a society will establish a great foundation. A country's joy arises from the peace and happiness of its people. The awareness of joy, the creation of joy, and the spreading of joy to the world, is part of the development of human character.

Giving others hope is of greatest importance to our present society. There is an ancient saying, "The saddest thing is no worse than the death of the heart (mind)." Hope is the inspiration for all achievement. Shakyamuni Buddha attained enlightenment and became a Buddha. The first message he shared with us was "Great! Great! All sentient beings on earth possess the Buddha's wisdom and virtue." This message provides all suffering beings with hope and benefit life after life.

To render service to people, one must use skillful means (Upaya) Of the Ten Paramitas, upaya is number seven. That means as a bodhisattva, we follow the conditions of all sentient beings, using various methods to teach and guide. In short, one should be flexible and know what to do at the most opportune moment. Upaya works with prajna. Knowing another's condition and level, we will be able to offer appropriate guidance. The principle of Buddha's Light members states: "If you think deeply, there will be deep reflection, and if you think in a shallow way there will be a shallow reflection. Only vows and practice can take us from the shallow to the deep."

## 2. The ideals of Buddha's Light members are expressed in four verses: "May honor return to the Buddha, may achievement belong to the majority, may benefit go to the monastery, and may merit go to the donor."

The above verses are the main focus of Buddha's Light members. The heart of belonging and contributing comes from the understanding that all sentient beings are one. If one does not know conditioned genesis, then one doesn't know the human world. In this world, time, space, and relationships are all like "Indra's net." They are endless. "From one grain of sand we can contemplate the whole world; from one drop of water we can contemplate the whole ocean; one is everything and everything is one." If there are no related conditions, then where do the benefits and merits come from? Everyone can return merits to the Triple

Gem if they understand conditions and know from where things come.

## 3. Beliefs of the BLIA

We respect and abide in the Triple Gem. The Dharma is eternal; Buddha's light shines everywhere.

We believe in humanistic Buddhism. We work to have productive lives and happy families.

We actively practice Buddhism with others. We show respect for others wherever we are.

We practice compassion, joy, and equanimity. Daily we do good deeds as we purify ourselves.

We respect all BLIA members. We welcome each other when we meet and acknowledge each other when we part.

We have right beliefs and right views. We discover Prajna wisdom deep inside ourselves.

We live in the peace and joy of the Dharma. We disentangle ourselves from suffering and ignorance.

We vow to save all sentient beings. We will make this world a Pure Land.

The relationship between Fo Guang Shan and the BLIA is very close. Fo Guang Shan represents the monastics, and the BLIA represents the lay Buddhists. Fo Guang Shan's modern organizational system is close to completion. We've developed international Buddhism, taught humanistic Buddhism, and improved the relationship between Mainland China and Taiwan. The BLIA provides devotees with many opportunities to teach the Dharma. It is through the cooperation of both monastics and lay people, that Buddhism permeates everyday life in the modern world. Using these methods, Buddhism will transcend nationality, ethnicity, and tradition.

We established the "Beliefs of the BLIA" so members would have standards to follow. First, we take refuge in the Triple Gem, and then we actively practice humanistic Buddhism by showing respect for others wherever we may be. The fifth belief defines interpersonal relationships. Belief seven asks all members to improve themselves and observe the precepts. Belief eight sets the ultimate goal for members of the BLIA and Fo Guang Shan, which is to establish a Pure Land in the present moment. All eight standards express a spirit of selfreliance and reliance on the Dharma. We can deeply experience life when we have these guidelines to follow; only then will we not lose our direction. These guidelines support the broadening of our views, opening of our hearts and making us willing to take on the responsibility of benefiting all sentient beings.

### 4. BLIA Verse

May kindness, compassion, joy, and equanimity pervade all Dharma realms.

May all beings benefit from our blessings and friendship.

May our ethical practice of Chan and Pure Land help us to realize equality and patience.

May we undertake the Great Vows with humility and gratitude.

*The Diamond Sutra* says that, "the virtue of following and practicing a four-sentence verse is greater than giving the seven treasures of the chiliocosm. That treasure cannot compare to the practice of only one verse."

The first two sentences, "May kindness, compassion, joy, and equanimity pervade all Dharma realms" and "May all beings benefit from our blessings and friendship" refers to the perfect connection in space, time, and relationship. The perfect application of our resources includes recycling and environmental protection. Protect all life with a compassionate heart, good intentions, and good behavior. Cherish one another.

The last two sentences are the core of the eight schools of Chinese Buddhism. It says in the *Avatamsaka Sutra* that the precepts are the supreme foundation for awakening. One should observe the full precepts with one's whole heart. Chan Master Yen Shou said, "Practiced together, Chan and Pure Land are like a tiger with horns. In this world you become a teacher to others, in the next world you will be among the Buddhas." If BLIA members practice Chan and Pure Land, they will be sure to improve the quality of their lives while increasing harmony among all with whom they come in contact. The BLIA verses possess four characteristics; the verses are standard, embody the highest virtues, are universal, and are in accord with the Dharma.

Buddha's Light members and BLIA members seem different because of the separation between a monastic and lay life. By outward appearances they look different, but in spirit and content you cannot have one without the other. It is like the two wings of a bird, or the two feet of a person. In short, whether you are a monastic or lay person the spirit and content are the same. The four great bodhisattvas are our role models and the prajna precepts are our teachers. Compassion, wisdom, vows, and practice are our inspiration. Awakening ourselves and awakening others is our goal.

### 1. In work we should:
A. Differentiate between that which is less important and that which is more important.
B. Share the resources. Practice teamwork.
C. Do not be over emotional. Be aware of your speech and contemplate your heart.
D. Do your duty. Be true in your work.

### 2. In our own practice and progress we should:
A. Practice kindness, compassion, joy, and equanimity; the four principles of guiding people (generosity, using encouraging language, having an accepting attitude, and including all beings in one's practice), and the Six Paramitas.

B. Study the teachings deeply. Have right understanding and right views.
C. Be pure and disciplined. Be content, and keep on the path.
D. Teach the eight schools and practice humanistic Buddhism. Our wish is that Buddha's Light members and members of the BLIA truly practice the above methods, beliefs, and ideals.

**Exercises:**

1. How do you practice the four Buddha's Light verses in your everyday life? Please give an example.
2. Describe the meaning of "honor belongs to the Buddha" and "achievement belongs to the majority."
3. Recite the Buddha's Light membership vow.
4. Explain the mutual relationship between Fo Guang Shan and the BLIA.
5. How should we emulate the spirit of the four great Bodhi-sattvas?
6. How do you maintain diligence in the effort to benefit others above oneself?

# Chapter 15
# The Social Actions in Humanistic Buddhism

*H*umanistic Buddhism emphasizes practice in our everyday life. The Buddha practiced in the human realm. Throughout many lives, he practiced generosity, befriended all, and ultimately attained Buddhahood. The Buddha was a pioneer in developing social actions in humanistic Buddhism. He had enough courage to destroy the caste system in India, and to propagate the idea of equality, proclaiming that all sentient beings possess Buddha Nature.

Today, society is in chaos. Many people feel disappointed and hopeless. Buddhism sustains peace and happiness, through advocating freedom from worry and fear. Fo Guang Shan and the BLIA have developed a series of Buddhist actions to aid in purifying their minds. The following is a list of the Four Good Actions.

**1. Rediscover Our Buddha Nature**

The present social order hastens the deterioration of morals and family values. Our lecture series increases societal understanding of this issue. Radio stations throughout Taiwan interview people from different careers. We produce educational films in Chinese and Taiwanese. We also cooperate with the *Central Daily News* by inviting people to write essays. We work with the various media to encourage society to care of our communities and families. As a beginning,, we should discover our own Buddha Nature. By using this boundless treasure and resource, we can help all sentient beings in finding the kindness, compassion, joy, equanimity, humility, and gratitude that they already possess.

The meaning of this program is to:
- A. Treasure life, be humble, and show gratitude.
- B. Respect nature and treasure our resources.
- C. Do not be greedy. Be content and possess the Seven Sacred Graces.
- D. Find our true nature and enjoy the wonder of it. Then we can enjoy the real beauty of life.

## 2. Seven Admonitions

The purpose of these admonitions is to purify people's minds, establish a harmonious society, stop the use of drugs, and to value ethics and morality. In this way, we can establish a peaceful and beneficial life.

The Seven Admonitions are:
- A. Abstaining from smoking and taking intoxicants
- B. Abstaining from sexual misconduct
- C. Abstaining from violence
- D. Abstaining from stealing
- E. Abstaining from gambling
- F. Abstaining from alcohol
- G. Abstaining from the use of harsh words

Our main activities in this area include assisting with drug rehabilitation programs, and encouraging everyone in the country to abide by these Seven Admonitions. We should do what we can to support this program. It is a long-term commitment with no end date. Through this effort, we can purify people's minds and support the country in riding itself of defilements.

The song of the Seven Admonitions says:
*When will social issues come to an end? Purifying people's minds is most important. If we follow the Seven Admonitions, then we know that chaos will disappear.*

*By abstaining from smoking and taking intoxicants we protect our lives. Health and longevity is our goal. If we can abstain from smoking and taking intoxicants, both family and society will improve.*

*By abstaining from sexual misconduct, there is no defilement. Couples will stay in love until the end of their lives. For teen prostitutes, we will protect and help them to help themselves. This is the bodhisattva path.*

*By abstaining from violence there is no anger, and everywhere harmony and courtesy will prevail. If we are tolerant, we can withdraw and create a space in order to enjoy good results.*

*By abstaining from theft and greed, contentment and joy will follow. By following this precept we will be prosperous. Having possessions cannot compare with knowing how to enjoy what we have.*

*By abstaining from gambling, we overcome greed. If we indulge in gambling, we become seized by the possibility of making more money. Thus we stay awake at night to gamble, sleep during the day, and do no productive work. Even if we earn money we will eventually lose our spouse and children.*

*By abstaining from alcohol and not getting drunk, we keep a clear mind. With a clear understanding, our body will feel healthy. This is the key to having a happy family.*

*By abstaining from harsh words, we avoid gossip. Giving words of encouragement is a wonderful method of avoiding gossip. By simply giving people joy and praise, the fragrance of the lotus will be everywhere.*

To raise life's standards we need to remember the Seven Admonitions. A Buddha's Light Pure Land relies on everyone working together in a positive way.

### 3. The Compassion and Love Program

Buddha's Light members all over the world are concerned about the social order getting worse, and want to prevent this tragedy from continuing. During a meeting at Fo Guang Shan, we decided to promote the "Compassion and Love Program." We encourage members to travel the whole island of Taiwan, teaching the Dharma on the streets, while spreading the seeds of compassion and love on every corner. In this way, they can bring brightness and hope to everyone.

There was a great response to this program. On the inauguration day, 80,000 people participated, and we asked everyone to take the "vow of compassionate love for people." Following the ceremony, there were two thousand compassionate teachers, committed to spending two hours a week in their community. They carried the flag and sang the "Song of Compassion and Love."

"To re-establish moral conduct, and re-enhance our families, our minds need to be purified. We need to search our consciences and be sincere in order to tame our society and love our country." Those who participated spread flyers of inspiring verses to especially reach out to the next generation. Participants promoted the Seven Admonitions, encouraging people to get rid of the Ten Evils by doing good deeds daily. For example, people can save one dollar each day to donate to charity work. They can make honest friends, do charity volunteer work, use the proper amount of money to live a normal life, teach people to benefit others, say good words, and feel joy for the good deeds of others. One can be a trustworthy person, do good deeds, and be perfectly willing to have a compassionate heart and always be joyful. In other words, people can use practical methods to practice compassion and love.

By starting with oneself and benefiting others, to purify our minds, establish good morals, and search our consciences, our society can be peaceful and joyous.

The goal of this activity is to:
  A. Bring compassion and love to the streets.
  B. Save our hearts and our country by encouraging all people to work together.
  C. Eliminate the Ten Evils, thereby enabling us to establish a happy family.
  D. Do good deeds daily, and together we can build a Pure Land.

## 4. Three Positive Solutions

There are many disorders in society that are due to the holding of incorrect values. There are those who use punishment to stop chaos. But serious punishment only produces temporary results. The real cure for this issue is to promote the concept of cause and effect. We use the Three Positive Solutions to promote this idea. The Three Positive Solutions are: do good things, say good words, and have a good heart. By using the Three Positive Solutions to overcome the Three Poisons, we can change violence to harmony, jealousy to praise, greed to generosity, and impurities to purity.

Upon submitting the idea of the Three Positive Solutions, the vice-president of the Republic of China immediately agreed to lead 100,000 people in making a vow to practice them. We need our bodies to do good deeds, our mouths to speak good words, and our minds to have good thoughts. If everyone follows these practices, our society will be filled with boundless beauty.

The meaning of this activity is expressed in the "Song of Three Positive Solutions:"

*The most beautiful things in the world are the Three Positive Solutions. One should be proud of oneself for learning them. Say good words, do good things, and have a good heart. The Three Positive Solutions are wonderful!*

*Listen! Saying compassionate and loving words are like the sun in the winter. Eencouragement and praise are like the blooming flowers. There is a sweet fragrance everywhere.*

*Look! Doing good things with your hands will create meritorious virtue. By rendering service you contribute to yourself, like the full moon shining in the sky.*

*Think! Having a good heart with sincere and good thoughts, good fortune will come to you. Your mind will emulate the sages, like the field that produces a bountiful harvest.*

*Taiwan, Taiwan! Taiwan is a precious island; let us work together to encourage everyone to learn the Three Positive Solutions. I say good words, you do good things, we have a good heart. Let everybody be good together. Peace is our gem in the world. The most beautiful thoughts in the world are the Three Soluions. To practice the Three Solutions is the most important activity.*

The social actions in humanistic Buddhism include the Four Positive Programs, as well as the annual worldwide Buddhist examination. This exam has guided a million people in learning more about Buddhism. To elevate morality, we teach in prisons, transmitting the precepts to the inmates. We communicate with those inmates who have committed serious offenses and assist with drug rehabilitation. These activities help the inmates in discovering the right path and how to eventually rejoin society.

The short-term monastic retreat, weekend practice, the Five Precepts, and the Bodhisattva Precepts are all long-term social actions in humanistic Buddhism.

The Buddha taught for forty-nine years. He taught kings,

ministers, merchants, farmers, women, children, and people of other religions. In this way, he used the social actions in humanistic Buddhism to purify people's minds.

**Exercises:**

1. Besides humanistic Buddhism social actions, please list other activities with a similar meaning.
2. List ten kinds of examples of "having a good heart".
3. List ten good sentences that you want to say.
4. List ten good things that you are able to do.

## Chapter 16
## Education and Training Concepts for Buddha's Light Members

*T*he Buddha was the greatest educator in the world, and Buddhism is what he taught. His teachings can help us perfect our lives. Monastics within the monastery need training in Buddhism, just as lay people and their children need to develop their beliefs by studying the Buddha's teachings. As Buddhists, we follow four stages: belief, understanding, practice, and realization. Whether we are a young person or an adult, we use these four methods of cultivation, secure in the knowledge that we all need to improve both our Buddhist practice and our learning.

### A. Belief

Belief is an inner treasure. Only with a right understanding of Buddhism can we receive the benefits. The following is a list of twenty ways in which practitioners can establish right belief.

1. Conditioned Genesis.

   The Buddha attained realization of the truth (awakening). This truth was conditioned genesis, which means that all things in the world arise through a combination of causes and conditions. All dharmas are examples of conditioned genesis.

2. Cause and effect.

   Everyone creates karmic causes that will eventually generate results. The arising of each result will set into motion a force that will become the cause of another result. This process of cause and effect is endless.

3. Wholesome and unwholesome karmic retribution.

   Do good and good will come to you; do bad and bad will come to you. Wholesome and unwholesome repayment arises from actions of the body, speech, and thought.

Wholesome and unwholesome karmic repayment is unaffected by "outside" powers.

4. Past life and future life.

   Buddhism refers to the three lifetimes of past, present, and future. The three lifetime cycles of rebirth are endless. They are also interrelated.

5. Impermanence.

   All things arise from causes and conditions. When conditions come together, something exists, and when conditions cease, it no longer exists. Everything is impermanent.

6. The true mind does not change.

   The true mind is Buddha Nature that is inherent in everyone. One person does not have more or less Buddha Nature than another. It is the same for everyone. Even while in other realms, the true mind stays the same.

7. The difference between sages and ordinary people.

   In the Ten Dharma Realms there are Four Sage Realms (Buddhas, Bodhisattvas, Pratyeka Buddhas, and Shravaka) and Six Ordinary Realms (heavenly, human, asura, animal, hungry ghost, and hell.) Within the Ten Dharma Realms, sentient beings have diverse causes and conditions; therefore their repayment will be different.

8. These four points are undeniable:

   A. Never doubt the Buddha's sacred teachings.

   B. Happily accept Buddhist truth.

   C. Diligently protect the monastic community.

   D. Sincerely follow Buddhist discipline.

9. When learning Buddhism one should:

   A. Have deep faith

   B. Pursue Buddhahood for oneself

   C. Save all sentient beings

   This will complete your practice

10. Do not slander the Dharma.

The Buddha attained enlightenment because of the Dharma, and the Sangha members accept the Dharma as their teacher. Within the Triple Gem, the Dharma is superior. The Dharma is the truth. With the help of the Dharma, we can guide sentient beings to freedom from the cycle of birth and death. When learning Buddhism, we should have deep faith and not slander the Dharma.

11. Right Understanding and Right View.

Develop both Right Understanding and a deeper awareness of Buddhism, so the proper benefit will be received.

12. Right Livelihood.

Diligence is the path toward success. Right Livelihood is the proper way to earn a living.

13. Praising the Triple Gem.

The Triple Gem: the Buddha, the Dharma, and the Sangha, help to save all sentient beings. We venerate the Triple Gem by offering our speech in praise.

14. Confidence and joy.

Be confident, joyful, and learn without doubt. Faith is the tool for entering the great ocean of the Dharma.

15. Inspiration and making vows.

Being perfectly willing to help is the way to develop mental treasure. Making vows will inspire us to achieve Buddhahood. When learning Buddhism, we should first focus on being perfectly willing and on making vows.

16. Do not forget initial intention.

Initial intention can keep the mind from forgetting that all things will be complete or accomplished.

17. Compassion and expedience.

Buddhism is built on the foundation of compassion. The expedient way is the path. Compassion can express Buddhism. Expedient ways are the tools of wisdom in dealing with worldly relationships.

18. Joining palms together and bowing.

    Joining palms means to join the secular and supramundane together and to follow the middle path. Worshiping (paying homage) is a way to communicate with the Buddha.

19. Life plan.

    For the first ten years, we should develop faith and understanding. For the second ten years we should travel, learn, and visit. For the third decade we should practice and make contributions. The fourth decade is for cultivating Chan and Pure Land practices. The fifth decade is for sharing our experience and teaching.

20. Passing faith to the next generation.

    Passing faith and all wholesome deeds to the next generation is the most valuable heritage.

## B. Understanding

The foremost activity when learning Buddhism is listening to the Dharma. By listening to the Dharma we can attain wisdom and truth. The following twenty points will help the practitioner with his approach to listening to the Dharma.

1. Prajna.

   Prajna is the foundation of the Six Perfections. Prajna is the source of all wholesome Dharmas. Prajna comes from listening, contemplation, and practice.

2. Developing an understanding of true meaning.

   Deeply understanding the Dharma is to realize the Buddha Nature within one's mind.

3. Listening to Dharma talks.

   The true teaching relies on hearing with a pure mind. Listening to the Dharma is the first step in believing in the teachings and entering the path. All merits in Buddhism come from listening to the Dharma.

4. Reading and studying the Tripitaka.

Read and study the Tripitaka. Study the sutras, the vinaya, and the shastras. We should study the works of the great historical masters in depth.

5. Being open-minded in listening.
In learning Buddhism we need to continually listen and learn many kinds of teachings.

6. Listening to and understanding the concept of emptiness.
The self-nature of all Dharmas is empty. Because of emptiness, we can establish everything. If we can properly understand the truth of conditioned genesis, then listening to the truth of emptiness will not frighten anyone. This is great wisdom.

7. Understanding wholesomeness and remembering it.

8. If one listens to wholesome words and does not remember them, that is not right thought. Listening to wholesome words and keeping them in mind, one will be ready to accept the Buddha's teachings.

9. Understanding the important points and contemplating them.

10. Listening carefully and understanding properly.
Listening to the Dharma, we need to constantly be mindful and contemplate. Only then can we open our minds and begin to understand. Listening to the Dharma, one needs to learn how to listen thoroughly and know how to open up to the true message.

11. Correctly listening and correctly contemplating.
Through listening, contemplating, and practicing the Dharma, one enters samadhi. Listen to the Dharma and memorize the teachings at all times.

12. Being optimistic and reasonable.
While learning Buddhism, one needs to understand causes, conditions, conditioned genesis, and emptiness. Only then can one be more optimistic, open-minded, wise, and reasonable.

13. Cultivating both merits and wisdom.
    To cultivate merit while not cultivating wisdom would be an imbalance. To cultivate wisdom while not cultivating merit would be like an arhat who receives no offering on alms rounds. Taking refuge in the Buddha means that we pay respect to the ones who have completed the practice of merits and wisdom.
14. Having good speech.
    By being compassionate and practicing wholesome words, one can speak correctly.
15. Teaching everywhere.
    Buddhism needs to be taught everywhere. Everyone will benefit.
16. Invitation to turn the Dharma wheel.
    Regularly attend Buddhist lectures, read Buddhist books, attend concerts, and special Dharma functions.
17. Associating with a monastery.
    Choose a monastery that appeals to you and associate with good Dharma teachers who can communicate well.
18. Spreading the Dharma protects Buddhism.
    Spreading the Dharma will guide others to the middle way and will eliminate all evil.
19. Protecting the Dharma.
    Support the development of Buddhist cultural and educational programs.
20. Eliminating evil and giving correct guidance.
    Eliminate evil and improve wrong behavior, wrong teaching, and wrong views to reveal the right Dharma and the right path.
21. Distinguishing right from wrong.
    Don't deliberate advantage and disadvantage or gain and loss. It should be clear through practice what is right and what is wrong.

## C. Practice

Even speaking the truth, the best of talk cannot compare with a solid practice. While learning Buddhism, one definitely needs to practice. Through practice, one can realize the truth.

The following thirty points concerning practice will aid the practitioner on the Buddhist path.

1. The Five Precepts and the Ten Wholesome Deeds provide the basis for being a good human being.

   By observing the Five Precepts and by following the Ten Wholesome Deeds, one can get good results and may be reborn in the heavenly or human realms.

2. Discipline.

   The precepts form the foundation for practice and the basis for liberation. Discipline is the path for security.

3. The Noble Eightfold Path:

   Right view

   Right understanding

   Right thought

   Right speech

   Right livelihood

   Right effort

   Right mindfulness

   Right concentration

4. The Four Immeasurable states of mind are:

   Kindness

   Compassion

   Joy

   Equanimity

5. The Six Paramitas are:

   Generosity

   Discipline

   Patience

   Diligence

   Meditation

   Wisdom

6. The expedient ways to guide people to Buddhism:
   Generosity
   Encouraging words
   Beneficial deeds
   Consideration
7. The four universal vows of a Bodhisattva:
   A. However innumerable sentient beings are, I vow to save them.
   B. However inexhaustible the defilements, I vow to eradicate them.
   C. However immeasurable the Dharmas are, I vow to master them.
   D. However difficult Enlightenment is, I vow to attain it.
8. The Four Contemplations:
   A. Contemplate the body as impure.
   B. Contemplate on all contaminated things being miserable.
   C. Contemplate the mind as impermanent.
   D. Contemplate on all phenomena as empty and without a self.
9. The Five Contemplations for overcoming defilements:
   A. Contemplation on impurity.
   B. Contemplation on compassion.
   C. Contemplation on conditioned genesis.
   D. Contemplation on the Buddha.
   E. Contemplation on the breath.
10. The four kinds of intensive practice:
    A. Generosity
    B. Offering
    C. Worship
    D. Chanting dharanis
11. The four kinds of reliances:
    A. Rely on the Dharma, not on the person
    B. Rely on wisdom, not on ones' knowledge

    C. Rely on the true meaning, not on words

    D. Rely on definitive teachings, not on interpretive teachings

12. Practice both Chan and Pure Land.

During the Song Dynasty, Yong Men Yen Sho said that, "With Chan and Pure Land one is like a tiger with horns. In this lifetime you will be a Dharma teacher. In the next life you can attain enlightenment."

13. Practice samadhi and vipassana.

When we cease distinguishing, cease all delusional thoughts, and concentrate on one point or objective, this is called samadhi. Having right understanding, contemplating all Dharmas, and recognizing all defilements is called vipassana.

14. Develop compassion and wisdom together.

Through compassion, one does not attach or bind to nirvana. Through wisdom, one does not attach to phenomena. By cultivating compassion and wisdom, one can save both oneself and others.

15. Treasure your good fortune and befriend all.

All merits are like savings in a bank; but the inherent merits are limited. However, the merits that you ac- cumulate can be endless.

16. Encouraging words.

Get along with people. Encouraging words are like sunshine, flowers, and pure water; they will be loved everywhere.

17. Patience and sensitivity.

Patience is recognition, the ability to take responsibility, and to be brave. If one has tolerance, then one can be sensitive.

18. Humility and repentance.

Humility is like clothing that can enhance our appearance. Repentance is like Dharma water that purifies our body

and mind.
19. Forgiveness.

As a Buddhist, one should not allow revenge to develop or accumulate. One should give others the opportunity to repent and improve.
20. Cultivate the six senses.

The six senses are like doors that are easily breached by the Six Dusts. As Buddhists, we should cautiously protect our six senses.
21. The Five Contemplations while having a meal:
    A. Be aware of how precious our meals are and learn to appreciate them.
    B. Assessing our virtues, are we deserving of the offerings of others?
    C. Guard against faults, greed in particular.
    D. A meal is like medicine, it gives us strength.
    E. Sustaining ourselves for spiritual cultivation, we need this meal. If you have the Five Contemplations, even gold is easy to digest. If you are deluded by the Three Poisons, even water is difficult to accept.
22. Pilgrimage:

By making pilgrimages to pay homage to the Buddha, we overcome our pride. By visiting others, we strive to befriend all.
23. Copying sutras and repenting:

Copying sutras can develop our wisdom.

Repentance can eradicate our negative karma and increase our merits.
24. Volunteer service:

To be a volunteer is to contribute our good intentions and life, and to give of our energy and time.
25. Protect the environment and protect life.

Protecting the environment is to protect the earth. Protecting lives is to respect life.

26. Worldly concerns:
   Regarding such things as clothing, food, making a living, transportation, and getting along with people, our manner should not be extravagant.
27. Contentment and gratitude:
   Being content is a good method we can use to be free from desires. Gratitude is our greatest asset.
28. Recognize mistakes and improve:
   By correcting one's mistakes, one can make progress. Recognizing one's mistakes, one can move forward.
29. Get rid of bad habits.
   We should develop the strength to get rid of bad habits in daily life, such as smoking and drinking.
30. Good bearing.
   Having good bearing is to walk like the wind, stand like a pine tree, sit like a bell, and recline like a bow.

**D. Realization.**

The world of religious experience after enlightenment is like drinking water. Only those who have drunk it can know the taste. To help in our Buddhist practice, the following twenty items are facets of the jewel that is enlightenment.

1. With right mindfulness, one will be free of delusion.
2. The true Dharma realm is one of equanimity and non-discrimination.
3. Contemplating our self-nature, all sentient beings can become Buddhas.
4. In attaining the realized middle path there is no birth, no arising, no distinguishing, no ceasing, and no continuation, no self, no others, no coming, and no going.
5. Get rid of delusion and mistakes and attain enlightenment.
6. One can achieve Buddhahood in this lifetime.
7. Body, speech, and thoughts are the masters of creating

karma. If we can purify the Three Karmas we can attain liberation.

8. After one passes away, one can be reborn in the Pure Land.

9. Transfer the five consciousnesses to wisdom of accomplishment; transfer the sixth consciousness to wisdom of discrimination; transfer the seventh consciousness to wisdom of equality; transfer the eighth consciousness to mirror-like wisdom.

10. Anytime and anyplace one can be liberated and carefree.

11. Wholeness and freedom are attaining the reality of the Dharmakaya. To enter nirvana and tranquility is the perfection of life.

12. Wonderful enlightenment is attained after completion of the fifty-two stages of the Bodhisattva enlightenment. Because this realm is so wonderful and incredible, it is called "wonderful enlightenment."

13. Supreme bodhi is the highest enlightenment.

14. True patience consists of life patience, Dharma patience, and the patience of the Supreme Dharma. The patience of the Supreme Dharma is the realization that the Dharma transcends birth, patience and all distinctions.

15. Four kinds of realized beings:
    A. Srota apanna
    B. Sakrdagami
    C. Anagami
    D. Arhat

16. Nirvana has two levels: nirvana with remainder and nirvana without remainder. By entering nirvana, one can escape from arising and ceasing, birth and death.

17. There are no differences between oneself and others. To realize that oneself and others are one is to realize the realm of enlightenment.

18. Realize the value of life and there is no fear of death.

Realize that birth and death transcend birth and death.

19. Defilements as bodhi. Purifying the defilements that the bodhi naturally presents is also a kind of liberation.
20. Non-attachment and right contemplation.
Right contemplation on phenomenoa is not clinging to defilements. Through non-attachment one can experience lightness and freedom.

The Buddha and his teachings are our only focus. The refinement of our character is our first and foremost responsibility. Hopefully, the cultivation of the above ninety items can provide a step-by-step guideline for Buddhists to use in their daily practice. With patience and diligence, these practices will enable Buddhists to have more complete and wholesome lives.

**Exercises:**
1. List five items that relate to beliefs.
2. List five items that relate to the practice of listening to the Dharma.
3. List five items that relate to practice.
4. List five items that relate to realization.

## Chapter 17
## Basic Questions Asked about
## Fo Guang Shan and the BLIA

1. **What is the focus of Fo Guang Shan?**
   A. To propagate all eight schools of Buddhism, and promote the coexistence of monastics and laity.
   B. To stress teamwork and promote respect and magnanimity.
   C. To attend equally to cultivating teaching, learning, and practice, and conduct business democratically.
   D. To have our monastery uphold the Six Harmonies and emphasize equality among the four groups (Bhiksu, Bhiksuni, Upasaka, Upasiksa)
   E. To harmonize politics, religion, and worldly affairs without conflict.
   F. To integrate tradition and modernism.
   G. To communicate globally, being conscious of homo- geneity and interdependence.
   H. To cultivate humanistic Buddhism to build a Buddha's Light Pure Land.

2. **What is the essence of Fo Guang Shan?**
   Nurturing talents through education.
   Propagating the Dharma through culture.
   Benefiting society through charity.
   Purifying people's minds through cultivation.

3. **When was Fo Guang Shan founded?**
   May 16, 1967.

4. **What is the meaning of "Fo Guang Year?"**
   A. The year that Fo Guang Shan was founded is used to,

commemorate the deeds that have been accomplished by the members.

B. To pray under the brilliance of the Buddha for equality, harmony, and wholeness to illuminate all Dharma realms.

C. To mark the time of important historical dates.

5. **What are the twelve rules for Fo Guang Shan monastic life?**

A. Monastics must keep a wholesome appearance by observing a regular grooming schedule.

B. Monastics are forbidden to build any personal temples.

C. Monastics are forbidden to spend any night outside a Buddhist temple.

D. Monastics are forbidden to make personal friends of devotees.

E. Monastics are forbidden to make monetary arrangements with anyone.

F. Monastics are forbidden to raise money for personal purposes.

G. Monastics are forbidden to transgress monastic ethics.

H. Monastics are forbidden to ask for personal favors.

I. Monastics are forbidden to recruit personal disciples.

J. Monastics are forbidden to purchase personal property.

K. Monastics are forbidden to accumulate personal savings.

L. Monastics are forbidden to prepare meals for themselves alone.

6. **What is the lineage of Fo Guang Shan?**

Fo Guang Shan belongs to the Lingi School of Chinese Chan Buddhism.

7. **What is the infrastructure of Fo Guang Shan?**

Besides forming a Religious Affairs Committee as the ultimate decision-making unit, Fo Guang Shan is made up of Five

Yuans and Ten Divisions. The Five Yuans are: the Senior Monastic, Supervising, Cultural, Educational, and Charitable. The Ten Divisions include: the Fo Guang Shan Sutra Revising and Editing Committee, Fo Guang Shan Cultural and Educational Foundation, Fo Guang Pure Land Cultural and Educational Foundation, Secular Cultural and Educational Foundation, Fo Guang Shan Sponsors' Association, International Buddhist Progress Society, Development Association of Buddha's Light International Association, Fo Guang Shan Higher Educational Preparative Committee, Fo Guang Shan Television Dharma Teaching Committee, and the Fo Guang Shan Religious Affairs Promotion Committee.

**8. What constitutes the supreme executive center of Fo Guang Shan?**

The supreme executive center of Fo Guang Shan is the Religious Affairs Committee which is made up of nine publicly elected members.

**9. What constitutes the personnel system of Fo Guang Shan?**

Personal experience

Monastics: Five orders and nineteen grades.

    A. Qing Qing Shi: Six grades, with each grade lasting for one year.

    B. Xueshi: Six grades, with each grade lasting from two to three years.

    C. Xiushi: Three grades, with each grade lasting from three to six years.

    D. Kaishi: Three grades, with each grade lasting from five to ten years.

    E. Senior Monastics

Qiaoshi, and Shigu: Consist of three orders and twelve grades.

    A. Qing Qing Shi: Six grades, with each grade lasting for one to three years.

B. Xueshi: Three grades, with each grade lasting from three to six years.

C. Xiushi: Three grades, with each grade lasting from five to eight years.

Decisions that are made at Fo Guang Shan and its related organizations are based upon the positions or rank held by individuals. On the one hand, the system honors and respects the experienced members so that seniority can be resspected within the Buddhist order. On the other hand, young talent is encouraged to bring vigor and flexibility to the system and to better facilitate the use of human resources.

## 10. What are the standards for promotion at Fo Guang Shan?

Academic Achievements: Secular diploma, Buddhist education, and sutra studies.

Work Contributions: Contribution of service to the temples and the length of service.

Cultivation: An individual's character, and morality.

## 11. How can one become a benefactor of Fo Guang Shan?

According to the by-laws of the Fo Guang Shan Benefactors'Association, individuals can be designated as benefactors if they fit into at least one of the following catagories:

A. They support and donate funds to promote various temple activities of Fo Guang Shan.

B. They have enthusiastically participated in the activities sponsored by Fo Guang Shan for many years.

C. They have devoted many years to temple service and believe resolutely in the Dharma.

D. They have contributed their wisdom and achievements to Fo Guang Shan.

E. They have assisted in the teaching of the Dharma and have been instrumental in the refuge taking of many individuals.

F. They have participated in the teaching of Buddhist beliefs and possess right views.

G. They have contributed to Dharma teaching through written words, especially publications.

### 12. How can one visit and practice at Fo Guang Shan?

Since its inception in 1967, Fo Guang Shan has allowed devotees to visit and cultivate their practice on the temple grounds. Even now devotees and the public can practice there. An application to visit can be submitted for approval by the headquarters or by any of the Fo Guang Shan branch temples.

### 13. How can one take part in "Weekend Retreats?"

Due to constant requests from lay devotees, the Religious Affairs Committee decided that beginning March 7, 1998, Fo Guang Shan would sponsor "Weekend Retreats." Numerous cultivation opportunities, including repentance, meditation, chanting, pilgrimages, sutra copying, Eight Precepts retreats, Buddhist lectures, volunteer meal preparation, family and youth camps, are regularly offered to interest lay devotees. To take part in these activities, both lay devotees and the general public can apply in person, or via the Internet, telephone, or fax at any Fo Guang Shan branch temple.

### 14. How can one visit the Monastery's Historical Museum?

Visitors who hold approved applications are welcome to visit.

### 15. Which departments at Fo Guang Shan frequently provide for lay devotee cultivation?

They are the Meditation, Pure Land, Sutra Copying departments and all of the units overseen by the temple. Lay devotees and the general public may register at the Visitor's Office of Fo Guang Shan or at any branch temple.

## 16. What has Fo Guang Shan achieved in spreading the Dharma?

By establishing many monasteries, both monastic and lay systems have been created, which serve as the foundation for cultural and educational affairs.

While developing a global Buddhism, many chapters of BLIA and Fo Guang branch temples have been established throughout the world. They form an important network which, sponsor international conferences to promote communication among the various schools of Buddhism.

Through the promotion of humanistic Buddhism, Dharma words serve as guiding ethics for everyday life. Many families have adopted and practiced the Dharma, facilitating the spreading of the Dharma to the general public.

To enhance communication between both sides of the Taiwan Strait and across the five continents, equality and mutual respect are stressed. Using mutual Buddhist affiliation and harmony builds a foundation of understanding.

## 17. How does Fo Guang Shan establish its branch temples?

Branch Temples are established in cities whose population numbers over one million.

Temple branches, lecture halls, or learning centers are established in cities that have populations of over two hundred thousand. The exterior of branch temples resemble that of a traditional temple, while lecture halls and learning centers are often situated inside of a modern city building.

Meditation Centers or Fo Guang Yuan are erected in counties or villages.

## 18. How many branch temples does Fo Guang Shan operate around the world?

Presently Fo Guang Shan operates 62 branch temples in Taiwan, and 98 throughout the rest of the world. (Fo Guang Yuan are excluded from these numbers.)

**19. What were the circumstances concerning the establishhment of these branch temples?**

By emulating the Buddha's conviction of spreading the Dharma over the whole of India, Fo Guang Shan has had to meet many difficult challenges as more than one hundred temples were built around the world. During this process, due to differences in cultures, traditions, and religious belief, Fo Guang Shan has encountered countless obstacles. Behind the establishment of each branch temple, there is almost always an unbelievable story of perseverance. For Instance, Hsi Lai Temple, the first branch temple in the United States, Nan Tian Temple in Australia, Nan Hua Temple in South Africa, Ho Hua Temple in Holland, Qile Temple in Keelung, Fa Pao Temple in Xianchu, Fu Shan Temple in Chang Hua, Yuan Fu Temple in Jia Yi, Huizu Temple in Shan Hua, and Fu Gao Temple in Tainan all have heartfelt stories of determination connected with their development.

**20. What are the development principles of Fo Guang Shan temples?**

A. To harmonize traditional and modern ways.

B. To demonstrate the coexistence of both monastics and laity.

C. To emphasize cultivation and understanding.

D. To integrate literary arts into Buddhism.

**21. How does Fo Guang Shan conduct its charity work?**

Since "utilizing charity to benefit society" is one of its four objectives, Fo Guang Shan has set up a Charity Yuan to handle all charity-related work. Within the Charity Yuan are the Charity Foundation, the Fo Guang Clinic, Yun Shui Mobile Hospital, Winter Assuagement Association, Catastrophe Relief Association, Friendly Service Team, Guan Yin Life Protection Association, Organ Donation Association, Social Service Center, Dazu Day Care Center, Lan Yang Nursery, Fo Guang Nursery, Wan Shou

Cemetery, and Senior Citizen Apartments. All of these institutions have been created to serve and care for both devotees' and the public's long-term life needs. In addition, branch temples around the world often sponsor charity campaigns, such as catastrophe relief, neighborhood friendship, and emergency assistance.

### 22. What does the Compassion Foundation of Fo Guang Shan do?

Based on the spirit of the Buddha: "compassion towards all beings and kindness towards mankind," Fo Guang Shan established the Fo Guang Shan Compassion Foundation. It includes welfare programs for the elderly, children, and the handicapped, medical subsidies for the poor, free medical services and care for low income families, emergency assistance, medical assistance for monastics, funeral assistance for the poor, management and development of volunteer work, and support for organ transplant.

### 23. What is the Yun Shui Mobile Hospital?

The Fo Guang Shan Mobile Hospital was established in 1976, originally under the name Fo Guang Shan Medical Care Team. Although free medical services were being provided to the poor, the Fo Guang Clinic could not reach people in remote villages where transportation was lacking. Using branch temples as bases, the Cloud and Water Mobile Clinic system was established to deliver needed medical care to these remote areas. Today there are more than twenty vehicles that serve as mobile hospitals, and more than a thousand people benefit each day from this free medical care.

### 24. What kind of services does Fo Guang Shan provide to the elderly and the young?

To promote the traditional spirit of filial piety, Fo Guang Shan has built the Lan Yang Ren Ai and the Fo Guang Home for the

Elderly. We also joined forces with the county government of Kaohsiung to establish the first public nursing home in Taiwan, the Feng Shan Home for the Elderly.

Fo Guang Shan's youth services are based on the spirit of "not only nurturing one's own youngsters but also others'." We fulfill that spirit through the services provided by Da Zu Nursery, Tainan Zu Hang Day Care, and Tainan Hui Zu Day Care Centers.

### 25. What is the current educational system of Fo Guang Shan?

"Use education to nurture talents" is one of the principles of Fo Guang Shan. Since its inception, Fo Guang Shan has vigorously moved toward this goal. Currently, our educational enterprises can be grouped into three main categories:

*Monastic Education* is provided for by sixteen Buddhist Colleges throughout the world.

*Social Education* is offered through five kindergartens, one elementary school, two secondary schools, four colleges, Shrimala Buddhist College, City Buddhist Colleges, and Fo Guang youth centers.

*Devotee Education* is provided through devotee seminars, staff seminars, volunteer seminars, short-term monastic retreats, Five Precepts and Bodhisattva Precepts retreats, as well as the World Buddhist Examination.

### 26. How many universities does Fo Guang Shan sponsor?

Fo Guang Shan sponsors the following four universities:

    A. Hsi Lai University in the United States, located in the Rosemead area of Los Angeles, California, was established in 1991. It is the first Buddhist University in California, and is also the first international university in the United States to be sponsored by Chinese Buddhists.

B. Nan Hua University of Jia Yi is located in Da Ling County in Jia Yi, Taiwan; R.O.C. Student recruitment began in the fall of 1996. It pioneered tuition exemption in order to give back to society and to those dedicated to learning.

C. Fo Guang University of Ilan is located on Ling Mei Mountain in Chiao Hsi, Ilan, Taiwan, R.O.C. The goal of this university is to provide students with a social education while placing emphasis on character development.

D. Fong Dao University is currently in the preparatory stage. It will be located in Hubei province in Mainland China.

### 27. How many secondary schools, elementary schools, and kindergartens has Fo Guang Shan established?

Joining forces with senior monks Nan Ding and Wu Yi, Fo Guang Shan erected Qi Guang Commercial Secondary School. Later, Pumen Secondary School was opened, offering junior high school, high school, and commercial high school classes. Today, Fo Guang Shan is preparing to open Ah Li Shan Secondary School. As for elementary schools, Fo Guang Shan operates Qun Tou Elementary School. In all, there are five kindergartens that are run by Fo Guang Shan: Zu Ai Kindergarten in Ilan, Zu Hang Kindergarten in Tainan, Hui Zu Kindergarten in Shan Hua, Pumen Kindergarten in Fo Guang Shan, and Xiao Tian Xing Kindergarten in Xin Ying.

### 28. How many Chinese schools has Fo Guang Shan established worldwide?

Fo Guang Shan erects its Chinese schools in branch temples around the world. In the United States, there are Chinese schools at Hsi Lai Temple in Los Angeles, California, the Learning Center in Denver, Colorado, Lian Hua Temple in Las Vegas, Nevada, and Fo Guang Shan New York Shrine. In addition, there are schools located in the Learning Center of Edmonton, Canada, Chung Tien Temple, Nan Tian Temple, Nan Tien Learning Center and Melbourne Learning Center of Australia, and the Chan Center of New Castle, South Africa. Besides assisting local Chi nese immigrants by teaching their children Chinese Mandrain language and traditional culture, they also serve as important sites for global cultural exchanges.

**29. What is the Devotee College?**

The Devotee College is located in Shanxia, Taipei, Taiwan, R.O.C. Being a Buddhist is the only requirement for admission to the college. Prepared and planned by the Fo Guang Shan Cultural and Educational Foundation, this college provides continuing education for devotees, and takes faith, understanding, practice, and validation as its themes of education. In the area of "understanding," the Devotee College offers instruction in Buddhist courses at all levels and seminars on secular knowledge and information technology. In the area of "practice," opportunities to practice in Chan, Pure Land, Tibetan Buddhism, and the precepts are offered without any preferential emphasis. Activities include meditation, chanting, sutra copying, sutra study, and pilgrimages. For continuing education, devotees can take short-term, long-term, and open schedule courses.

**30. How many Buddhist Colleges have been established worldwide by Fo Guang Shan?**

At present, Fo Guang Shan has set up sixteen Buddhist colleges throughout the world which include: Chinese Buddhist Study College, Fo Guang Shan English Buddhist College International Division, Japanese Buddhist College, Foreign Student Study Classes, Fo Guang Shan College Women's and Men's Sections, Jilong Women's Buddhist College, Fu Shan Buddhist College, Ping Dong and Shramanera campuses of

Eastern Buddhist College, Hsi Lai Buddhist College -United States, Dong Chan Buddhist College Malaysia, Africa Buddhist College, Nan Tian Buddhist College Australia, Hong Kong Buddhist College, and India Buddhist College.

### 31. How does one apply for admission to a Fo Guang Shan Buddhist College?

One may register in person at any branch temple, through the Internet, or by telephone.

### 32. What is the Shramanera Campus?

Established in 1967, Fo Guang Shan Shramanera Campus admits boys who have graduated from elementary school. The aim of the curriculum is to foster an understanding of Buddhist concepts, combined with the practice of Buddhism. The courses that are offered include studies in basic Buddhist knowledge, everyday life, Chinese and other languages, and computer technology. Students participate in the schools daily operations through serving meals and other duties in order to develop tolerance and friendship in their relationships and to cultivate merits through their work. In addition, reciting dharani, making pilgrimages, meditating, and diary writing are all courses that aim to develop students' reflection and mindfulness. Upon completion of their studies at Shramanera Campus, students may continue their studies at the Men's College.

### 33. What are the current cultural activities at Fo Guang Shan?

With regard to cultural activities, Fo Guang Shan has a Sutra Compilation Department, Awaken the World Monthly Journal Publishing House, Universal Gate Journal Publishing House, Fo Guang Shan Cultural Enterprise Corporation, Fo Guang Shan Video and Audio Center, Fo Guang Bookstore, Gift Shop, Fo Guang Yuan Art Museum, Hsiang Hai Cultural Enterprise

Company, and Thus Have I Heard Cultural Enterprise Company. All of these cultural institutions continuously publish and compile various books and journals, as well as provide books, paintings, audiotapes, CDs, and videotapes. Fo Guang Shan's cultural programs take the responsibility of spreading the Dharma to the public.

### 34. What are the contents and characteristics of the Fo Guang Tripitaka?

Due to the vast number of Buddhist terms in traditional sutras, non-scholars despite their eagerness to learn, encounter great difficulty in their mastery of the Dharma. In 1977, Fo Guang Shan established the Fo Guang Buddhist Sutra Compilation and Rectification Council, employing Venerable Master Hsing Yun as chairperson. He assembled monastic and lay scholars to organize, correct, and interpret ancient Buddhist sutras. While adding bibliographies and notes for each of the sutras, they came up with the idea of producing a set of Buddhist "scriptures." As definitive Buddhist texts, the public can now understand and practice the Dharma with confidence. With this tool, the Dharma can be spread far and wide.

In the "Fo Guang Tripitaka," sutras are arranged into sixteen different groups, including: Agama Canon, Prajna Canon, Chan Canon, Pure Land Canon, Lotus Canon, Avatamsaka Canon, Lankavatara Canon, Esoteric Canon, Shravaka Canon, Vinaya Canon, Original Phenomenon Canon, Historical Legend Canon, Painting Canon, Etiquette Canon, Art Canon and Literary Canon, and Miscellaneous Canon. Currently, seventeen volumes of Agama Canon, 51 volumes of Chan Canon, 42 volumes of Prajna Canon, and 33 volumes of Pure Land Canon have been completed. Since their publication, these books have been donated to universities, and other educational institutes, and academic agencies, libraries, scholars and professors, Buddhist organizations, temples, and to media outlets worldwide. Critical reviews and reader responses have thus far been very positive.

### 35. What are the characteristics of the Chinese Buddhist Sutra Treasure?

The Chinese Buddhist Sutra Treasure comprises a set of 132 volumes. The sutras that were selected contain deep historical meaning that has impacted Chinese culture, and the ideology of humanistic Buddhism. Each volume contains an introduction to the subject, its origins, and interpretation of the sutra. The interpretation describes the historical background and value of the sutra, its role in Buddhist history and in the evolution of its thought. Beyond its value in popular literature and for academia, this treasure sutra has also been a pioneer in four areas:

A. This is the first such collection in Buddhist history.

B. It is the result of the cooperative efforts of distinguished scholars.

C. It offers the possibility of an exchange of the Dharma between Taiwan and Mainland China;

D. It offers the best collection of popular Buddhist sutras. This set preserves an excellent collection of Buddhist sutras that are of great historical significance in the development of Chinese Buddhism.

### 36. How many libraries has Fo Guang Shan established around the world?

The libraries that have been established by Fo Guang Shan include Hsi Lai University Library, Nan Hua University Library, Xinzhu Wu Liang Shou Library, Fo Guang Shan Public Library, Da Zu Library, Ta Tzu Day Care Children's Library, Buddhist College Research Center, Men's Section Library, Women's Section Collective Library, and the International Learning Library. There are sixteen Buddhist college libraries, as well as branch temple libraries of Fo Guang Shan including Hsi Lai Temple in the United States and Nan Tian Temple in Australia.

### 37. Why did the Fo Guang Buddhist Encyclopedia win the "Golden Kettle Award" in the best book category?

In 1977, the Compilation and Correction Committee of the Fo Guang Tripitaka assembled more than twenty people from the Fo Guang Shan Chinese Buddhist Research College. We also recruited scholars who were adept in the Dharma, literature, history, philosophy, and languages such as Sanskrit, Pali, English, and Japanese. This edition, the publication of which was overseen by Venerable Tzu Yi, consists of eight volumes containing 7,000,000 words and took ten years of dedicated effort to complete. A unique feature of this encyclopedia lies in its clear interpretation of profound Buddhist philosophy that is supplemented with related illustrations. General Buddhist terminology, names of people, cities and temples, Buddhist sectarian teachings, sutra phrases, rituals involving the use of Buddhist musical instruments, Buddhist art, and Buddhist legends are all cataloged and explained in detail. In addition, an index volume has been published making reference more accessible to readers. Every entry in the encyclopedia, whether it relates to recent or ancient times, is recorded in great detail. The encyclopedia's references cover thousands of sutras and books, and its interpretations and discussions have been gathered from numerous authorities. This encyclopedia is definitely a Buddhist treasure for the people of today.

## 38. What roles do the Fo Guang Bookstore and the Gift Shop play in spreading the Dharma?

To make it convenient for devotees to purchase Buddhist books, ritual items, and audio and video tapes, Fo Guang Shan has set up Gift Shops and Fo Guang Bookstores at each branch temple, in different cities around the world. These stores not only initiate and motivate exchanges of Buddhist merchandise throughout the world, but also spread Buddhist culture and teachings.

## 39. What is the Xiang Hai Cultural and Business Corporation?

Established in 1997, Xiang Hai Cultural and Business Corporation, working with the Fo Guang Publishing Company, has served as a bridge between Buddhist culture and societal communications. All of the published Buddhist books, audio and videotapes, and cultural merchandise are widely distributed through Xiang Hai Corporation. This process affords the general public an opportunity to come into contact with Buddhism.

**40. How does the "Thus Have I Heard" Cultural Corporation promote Buddhist music?**

Established in 1997, the "Thus Have I Heard" Cultural Corporation acquired its name with the hope of emulating the dedication of Venerable Ananda in spreading the Dharma, through broadcasting and producing high quality Buddhist music. It is the company's wish to use such music to purify society and to improve the conditions of both mind and body.

**41. What are the contributions of Fo Guang Shan in promoting humanistic Buddhism?**

Fo Guang Shan is:

A. Increasing the number of practicing Buddhists around the globe.

B. Promoting the learning of the Dharma among today's youth.

C. Enabling lay Buddhists to spread the Dharma.

D. Increasing the value and appreciation of Buddhism through the media.

E. Making Buddhist cultural merchandise widely available.

F. Promoting Buddhist music worldwide.

G. Developing the BLIA.

H. Generating the interest of educational institutions in Buddhism.

I. Bringing Buddhist practice to political leaders. Enabling popular entertainers to take refuge in Buddhism.

J. Being responsible for the promotion of the Buddhist World Examination.

K. Spreading the Dharma beyond national borders.

## 42. What has Fo Guang Shan done to expand social education?

Tasks that Fo Guang Shan has undertaken in the area of social education are the World Buddhist Examination, Dharma teaching in prisons, Buddhist precepts revising class, Rediscovering our Buddha Nature, the Seven Admonitions, Training Program for Compassionate and Kind-hearted People, the Three Positive Solutions, establishing radio stations, Fo Guang Yuan Art Museum, and various Buddhist and art classes sponsored by Fo Guang Yuan. The purpose of all of these activities is to assist and support the purification of minds and strengthen social consciousness.

## 43. What are the Fo Guang Yuan?

To make the saving of all sentient beings more possible, and to provide ample opportunities for the general public to become involved in Buddhism, all of the activities that Fo Guang Shan coordinates and sponsors are called Fo Guang Yuan. Examples of such activities are the establishment of bookstores, art museums, teahouses, and teaching institutes, as well as the holding of fairs and auctions.

## 44. Where did the idea for the teahouse come from?

The meaning behind the teahouse comes from "repaying generously for a tiny amount of aid from others." It provides the opportunity to meet with friends. The teahouse began in 1994 when the Fo Guang Yuan Art Museum was established. To show appreciation to the public, Fo Guang Shan opened a teahouse near the museum to provide devotees with a place to rest and relax after visiting. Currently, there are Fo Guang Shan teahouses in every corner of the world for the convenience of devotees.

### 45. What foundations does Fo Guang Shan support?

The Fo Guang Shan Educational and Cultural Foundation, the Fo Guang Pure Land Educational and Cultural Foundation, Fo Guang Shan Compassion Society Welfare Foundation, Secular Educational and Cultural Foundation, and the Fo Guang Shan Television Teaching Foundation are all foundations that are supported by Fo Guang Shan.

### 46. What is the Fo Guang Satellite Television Station?

Today, both radio and television have become very important tools for teaching the Dharma. Aware of this trend, Fo Guang Shan established the Fo Guang Satellite Television Station in November 1996, and began broadcasting on January 1, 1998. Pioneering a format without interruptions by commercial advertising, the Fo Guang Satellite Television Station produces programs relating to Buddhism, education, history, youth, and women. These programs have created a refreshing television Pure Land in today's world of "flashy" audio and video. In its first year of operation, the station won awards for Best Editing and Best Host of a Cultural Program in the 34th Television Golden Bell Awards, and was also the first and sole winner of the National Satellite Television Stations award of Taiwan.

### 47. How can one contact Fo Guang Shan?

By telephone, Fo Guang Shan can be reached at 011-886-7-6561921-8. The Website address of Fo Guang Shan is www.fgs.org.tw.

### 48. Who are Fo Guang members?

By definition, all past, current, and future Buddhist monastics, and lay followers of Fo Guang Shan will be called Fo Guang members. However, all of those who approve of the Dharma work that is undertaken by Fo Guang Shan may be called Fo Guang members.

**49. How can one know Fo Guang Shan?**

Study the entire foundation of Fo Guang Shan, not just its outward appearance. Observe all of the people who are part of Fo Guang Shan, not just a few members. Examine the entire system of Fo Guang Shan, not just its individual parts. Inspect the whole history of Fo Guang Shan, not just one moment.

**50. How is Fo Guang Shan developing a global, systematic, modern Buddhism that reaches out to all sentient beings?**

Globalization: The Dharma has no national boundaries. To allow "the Buddha's light to shine everywhere, and the Dharma waters to flow to all continents," Fo Guang Shan has established many temples throughout the world. Also, the BLIA can now be found in more than 130 countries. In addition, young people from eighteen countries such as India, Sri Lanka, and South Africa are studying in the Buddhist Colleges of Fo Guang Shan, and scholars from about ten countries are now exploring special subjects there as well. In this regard Fo Guang Shan is a prosperous, miniature version of the United Nations. Under the ideals of ethnic and cultural harmony, Fo Guang Shan is strenuously working toward the globalization of Buddhism.

Systematization: As Fo Guang Shan is a monastery that values a systematic approach, its network is elaborate. For example, reward and correction, promotion and relocation, finance and accounting, the taking of monastic precepts, the construction of temples, even the rules and regulations of the monastery and of the monastics' continuing education and benefits, are all part of a well-defined system of management.

Modernization: Fo Guang Shan persists in carrying out a traditional life of cultivation, but it utilizes modern methods of teaching the Dharma. For example, by using television, radio, and publishing, Fo Guang Shan seeks every opportunity to allow Buddhism to reach every family. We promote the integration of the Dharma into everyday life, and for everyday life to reflect the Dharma.

Reaching out to the world: Fo Guang Shan promotes a Buddhism that is based on human needs. To this end, we actively send forth the Dharma from the temple into society and from monastics to lay followers.

**51. A description of the Honorary Board of Fo Guang Shan.**

Fo Guang Shan has nearly two thousand monastics who have endeavored and earned recognition in cultural activities, education, and charity work during the past thirty years. For instance, Venerable Tzu Zhuang is an honorary citizen of Los Angeles. Venerable Tzu Hui won an award for her Taiwanese social work. Venerable Hsin Ting was a winner of a social education award that was given by the Ministry of Education of Taiwan. Venerables Tzu Jung, Xiao Chueh, and Yung Sheng have won several times as the "Representative of National Good Deeds and Good People Award of Taiwan". Venerable Yi Jung was the winner of the "Nan Yang Distinguished People Award." Venerable Tzu Yi won the "Golden Kettle Award in Publishing" which was a first for Buddhist books. Venerable Yi Kung won an "Excellence in Culture Building" award for promoting Buddhist Culture in Taiwan. Venerable Yi Fa won the "Ten Distinguished Youth Award" in Taiwan. Venerable Huei Kai received the "National Social Excellence Youth Award" of Taiwan. Venerable Yi Lai won the recognition of the Australian government and the "Contribution to Community Service Award." Venerable Yi Qian, who has dedicated herself for years to child education, won the "Example of Child Education and Service Award." Venerable Yi Hua won the "Distinguished Student Award" from the Tibetan Buddhist College. In addition, there are more than ten monastics who hold Doctorates and nearly a hundred have Masters degrees.

**52. What recent international meetings have been sponsored by Fo Guang Shan?**

Since its inception, Fo Guang Shan has devoted itself to the task of making Buddhism a truly global religion. To this end, it has sponsored numerous meetings, such as the International Buddhist Meeting, Global Buddhist Youth Conference, World Sutric and Tantric Buddhist Conference, International Chan Conference, Friendship Meeting of World Buddhists and World Buddhist Youth. We have also sponsored the International Distinguished Buddhist Women Meeting, the World Distinguished Buddhist Men Meeting, International Buddhist Monastics Seminars, First International Catholic and Buddhist Communication, International Electronic Buddhist Tripitaka Conference, and International Conference of Asian Religion and Higher Education.

## 53. Who are the "Hundred Renowned People" of Fo Guang Shan?

Behind the Main Shrine and in front of the Tathagata Hall of Fo Guang Shan, there is a collection of famous Chinese historical figures; literary giants such as Dao Yuan Ming, Wang Wei, Liu Zong Yuan, Lu Yu, painters and calligraphers like Su Dong-Bo, Dong Qi-Chang, Cheng Pan-Qiao, Feng Ze Kai, Yu Yu-Ren, and Chang Da-Qian, and the great Buddhist masters Huai Su, Han Shan, Shi De, Hai Su, Dao Yuan, Yong Ming Ye Shou, De Qing, and Ze Bo. There are a total of a hundred inspiring and educational exhibits as well as the "Great Compassion Painting" that is carved on black gemstone as well as the first Buddhist mural carved in marble. This collection officially opened on May 16, 1996.

## 54. What is the purpose of sponsoring a Fo Guang Relatives Meeting at Fo Guang Shan?

Once every two years, Fo Guang Shan sponsors the "Fo Guang Relatives Meeting." This event has four purposes:

A. To build a Buddhist ethics;

B. To strengthen communications between monastics and lay followers;

C. To enhance our relatives' understanding;

D. To promote harmony in the secular world.

# Basic Questions asked about Buddha's Light International Association (BLIA)

## 1. When did the Buddha's Light International Association (BLIA) form?

The BLIA, Republic of China Chapter was officially inaugurated on February 3, 1991. An inaugural conference was held at the Dr. Sun Yat-sen Memorial Hall in Taipei, Taiwan, ROC. The BLIA World Headquarters was formed on May 16, 1992 at the Los Angeles Music Center in, California, USA.

## 2. What kind of an organization is the BLIA?

The BLIA is an organization of laypersons that promote the internationalization of Buddhism. It stresses strong cooperation between Buddhist monastics and lay followers in activities that range from cultivation through religious services to participation in social activities, from the formation of Buddhist groups to fostering communication with all religious groups. Thus, the BLIA is an organization that embraces compassion and kindness, promotes equality among all sentient beings, respects family life, and emphasizes social welfare.

## 3. What is the origin of "BLIA Day?"

When BLIA members held the beginning conference for the BLIA World Headquarters at the Los Angeles Music Center in Los Angeles on May 16, 1992, they decided that May 16th would henceforth be known as "BLIA Day", allowing members to celebrate this historic event. Meanwhile, the Mayor of Monterey Park, California, Mr. Chiang Kuo-liang, responded favorably and declared May 16th "BLIA Day" in the city of Monterey Park.

## 4. How does the BLIA relate to Fo Guang Shan?

Fo Guang Shan is an organization for monastics, while the

BLIA is for lay devotees. These two develop together, supporting one another, and shouldering the responsibility of educating all sentient beings. Fo Guang Shan is a group member of the BLIA, fully supporting all BLIA sponsored activities. The BLIA are the Dharma Protectors of Fo Guang Shan, fully supporting the various activities for spreading the Dharma.

**5. What was the reason for starting the BLIA?**

The purpose of starting the BLIA was to provide all Buddhist followers with the opportunity to become involved in the spreading of the Dharma, using the united power of both the monastic community and lay disciples. The BLIA was founded to meet the challenges of internationalizing Buddhism, adapting Buddhism to a modern form that meets the needs of today's world, is relevant to everyday life, and transcends nationality, ethnicity, and creed. The goal of the BLIA is to allow the Buddha's light to shine everywhere and Dharma waters to flow throughout the whole world.

**6. What are the guiding principles of the BLIA?**

The BLIA was founded on a belief in the teachings of the Buddha, on a respect for the Triple Gem (the Buddha, Dharma, and Sangha), and on the interest in teaching the Dharma for the benefit of all sentient beings.

As BLIA members, we must advocate a living Buddhism that seeks to make a Pure Land of this world. Our focus is to teach the Dharma in this world and to practice compassion for the benefit of this world. We must revere the practices that have been bequeathed to us by the Buddha. We must complete the development of our character by practicing the Three Learnings: (morality, meditation, and wisdom).

As BLIA members, we must cultivate a broad-minded character, one capable of embracing all cultures and societies of the world. We must publish books and magazines, teach, and do what is necessary to bring the Dharma to its fullest fruition. We must always be willing to open our hearts and do whatever we can to aid and support others.

7. **What are the aims of the BLIA?**
   A. To advocate humanistic Buddhism.
   B. To seek to purify the mind.
   C. To seek to establish a Pure Land in this world.
   D. To work toward the goal of world peace.

8. **What are the principal responsibilities of the BLIA?**
   A. To encourage the study of Buddhism and the production of Buddhist literature.
   B. To take on social responsibilities and expand educational opportunities.
   C. To develop Buddhist education and to nurture people's talents.
   D. To promote the internationalization of the Dharma.

9. **What keynote speeches has the BLIA published?**
   Since its establishment in 1992, the BLIA has sponsored an annual general conference for members, utilizing a keynote speech as both a spiritual guide and as a direction for future endeavors. Previous keynote speeches include "Joy and Harmony," "Respect and Tolerance," "Equality and Peace," "Wholeness and Freedom," and "Nature and Life."

10. **What are the benefits of joining the BLIA?**
    A. To meet emotional needs for community and com- panionship.
    B. To expand our study and learning.
    C. To fulfill professional and personal growth.
    D. To bring joy in celebration and comfort in times of sadness.

E. To encourage family life and its benefits.

F. To educate children to live productive and moral lives.

G. To travel the globe and meet people from other cultures.

H. To join activities and purify our minds.

I. To vow to do good and avoid that which is not good.

J. To practice together and transcend difficulties.

K. To hear the Dharma and receive blessings.

L. To open up to our unlimited potential.

**11. How does one become a BLIA member?**

The following is the way to become a member in the BLIA. First, take part in BLIA sponsored activities in order to understand the ideals of the BLIA and to recognize the spirit of the BLIA. Next, get references from two current BLIA members and uphold the vows of the BLIA.

**12. What does the ceremony of joining the BLIA involve?**

The ceremony for new BLIA members includes the recitation of the following vow:

"I will sincerely observe the guiding principles legislated by the BLIA World Headquarters, and will follow the by-laws established by the World Headquarters and my local chapter. Based on the teachings of the Buddha, I will revere the Triple Gem and follow the tenets of humanistic Buddhism. I will balance learning and practice to cultivate both wisdom and compassion, wishing to be awakened and to awaken others to be self-sufficient, helpful to others, and to benefit all sentient beings."

**13. How can one be a good member of the BLIA?**

A. As a global being, coexist with all beings.

B. As a compassionate being, unite with all beings.

C. Be a clear-sighted and wise person.

D. Be patient and learn to endure.

E. Learn to give.

F. Purify one's mind through practice.

G. Be joyful.

H. Broaden one's community.

**14. What should BLIA members strive for?**

A. To think of ourselves and others as global beings in common.

B. To humanize Buddhism.

C. To have a vision in facing the future.

D. To base unity on clear guidelines.

**15. What are the "Four Verses of the BLIA?"**

*May kindness, compassion, joy, and equanimity pervade all Dharma realms;*

*May all beings benefit from our blessings and friendship;*

*May our ethical practice of Chan and Pure Land help us to realize equality and patience;*

*May we undertake the Great Vows with humility and gratitude.*

**16. What are the "Four Pillars of Goodness" for BLIA members?**

A. Purify one's mind.

B. Consider one's use of language.

C. Do good things.

D. Be a good person.

**17. What is the spirit of BLIA members?**

A. The four great Bodhisattvas are our models.

B. The eight Supernatural Beings are our guardians.

C. The four Diamond Dharma Protectors are our strength.

D. The Buddhas of the ten directions are our ideals.

**18. What are the obligations of BLIA members?**

A. Identify and recognize the guiding principles and aims of the BLIA and promote them widely.
B. Support the organization and activities of the BLIA.
C. Attend meetings and pay the annual membership dues.
D. Faithfully uphold the bylaws and rules of the BLIA.

**19. What are the duties of BLIA members?**
A. Teach the Dharma to the world.
B. Promote humanism.
C. Benefit all sentient beings based on compassion.
D. Distinguish between right and wrong.

**20. What are the benefits of becoming a member of the BLIA?**

Within the BLIA, one has the right to vote, to be elected as a staff member, to speak, and to decide issues concerning the organization. One also can receive magazines that are published by the BLIA. Members also assist other members with weddings and funerals. While traveling to other parts of the world, BLIA members can enjoy the services that Fo Guang Shan branch temples offer. By passing the qualification examinations, one can serve as a lay Dharma teacher for the BLIA.

**21. What ideals and aims does the BLIA have in establishing its system of lay Dharma teachers and instructors?**
A. To expand the spread and influence of Buddhism.
B. To establish ethics and order within the organization.
C. To practice equality in Buddhist teachings and within the monastery.
D. To achieve harmony and mutual respect between monastics and lay followers.

**22. How can BLIA members become lay teachers?**
A. Have right understanding and right views.

B. Believe in Buddhist precepts, meditation, and wisdom.

C. Believe in cause and effect.

D. Hold a strong sense of community.

E. Practice compassion and purity.

F. Practice virtue.

G. Practice skillful means.

H. Have clear verbal abilities.

I. Have reverence.

J. Be sincere in tone of voice.

K. Uphold the five precepts.

L. Promote a joyous family environment.

### 23. How can BLIA members build contented families?

BLIA members can build contented families by being temperate in their emotions, reasonable in their social lives, moderate in their economic practices, and ethical in their religious lives. Husbands and wives should have mutual respect and consideration for each other, let each other know their whereabouts, attend social functions as a couple, carry little money, and keep no secrets.

### 24. How do BLIA members educate their children?

A. By instilling a receptive and open attitude.

B. By teaching good manners.

C. By practicing respect for life.

D. By stressing industriousness.

E. By emphasizing gratitude.

F. By teaching the Dharma.

G. By teaching the cultivation of a stable personality.

H. By instilling a strong belief in the Dharma.

### 25. How do BLIA members plan their lives?

By emphasizing the advancement of belief, listening to the Dharma, making associations through giving, participating in group cultivation, and doing volunteer work.

By enhancing understanding, studying and reading biogra phies, Buddhist history, special books on Buddhist schools, and exploring Buddhist sutras.

By stressing the content of practice, chanting the names of the Buddha, meditating, chanting sutras, practicing repentance, volunteering, and supporting the Dharma.

By assisting the propagation of the monastery, passing down experiences, helping development, sponsoring activities, and upholding the precepts.

If BLIA members have plans for their lives, they can contribute to the organization, serve as good examples to others, and bestow a legacy of teachings and achievements.

### 26. What type of practice should a BLIA member have?

BLIA members should recite the "Four Verses of the BLIA" before meals, practice Buddha's Light samadhi regularly, participate in various Dharma services held by the temple, and set up a program of personal practice.

### 27. What is Buddha's Light samadhi practice?

Buddha's Light samadhi is a routine practice for every BLIA member, incorporating current and ancient practices that are suitable for modern times. It is composed of four parts: praying, chanting, meditation, and practice.

### 28. What special forms of etiquette do BLIA members practice?

Prior to any BLIA meetings, the members sing the "Ode to the Triple Gem" and recite the "BLIA Members' Guidelines." At the conclusion of meetings, the members sing the "BLIA Anthem."

### 29. What are the BLIA Members' Guidelines?

A. Respect and abide in the Triple Gem. The Dharma is etenal.

The Buddha's light shines everywhere.

B. Believe in the principles of humanistic Buddhism. Work to have good lives and happy families.

C. Actively practice Buddhism with others. Show respect for others wherever we are.

D. Practice compassion, joy, and equanimity. Do good deeds and purify one's mind daily.

E. Respect all BLIA members. Welcome each other when meeting and acknowledge each other when parting.

F. Have right beliefs and right views. Discover the Prajna wisdom deep inside oneself.

G. Live in the peace and joy of the Dharma. Disentangle oneself from suffering and gnorance.

H. Vow to save all sentient beings and make this world a Pure Land.

**30. How can members express the meaning of the "BLIA Anthem" while singing it?**

At the conclusion of each BLIA meeting, members should sing the "BLIA Anthem." Since this song denotes the spirit of the organization, we should sing our guiding principles of "undertaking teaching the Dharma to benefit all beings" with emotion and sincerity. We should sing our belief of "differentiating right from wrong" with a strong voice. We should sing our spirit of "emulating the four great Bodhisattvas" with solemnity. We should sing of our hope to "build a Pure Land" with joy. We should sing of our vision to "benefit society and see the whole world" with clarity. We should sing of our long-term aim to "exist as one and embrace the world" with a solid voice. We should sing of our great vow that "the Buddha's light shines everywhere, the Dharma water flows forever" with a sustained voice. Buddhist music is capable of saving others. We should endeavor to express the meaning of the "BLIA Anthem" through singing, making Buddhism accessible to all, thus allowing the Dharma to be widely accepted.

### 31. What is the meaning of the BLIA symbol?

The BLIA symbol is representative of the spirit of our organization. It has the following meaning:

A. The circle symbolizes wholeness without hindrance. The lotus flower symbolizes pure Bodhi.

B. The circle symbolizes this saha world. The lotus flower symbolizes the transcendental truth, which grows out of this world.

C. The circle symbolizes our inherent Buddha Nature, waiting to be fully developed. The lotus symbolizes enlightenment within the wisdom of the Buddhas.

D. The circle symbolizes the earth. The lotus symbolizes the Buddha's light.

### 32. What does the BLIA lotus gesture mean?

When BLIA members meet, they use two gestures as greeing:

A. The first gesture is turning the palm out while the thumb touches the middle finger, keeping the other three fingers outward. This gesture denotes welcome, acceptance, fellowship, reflection, and purity.

B. The second gesture is the lotus clasping of hands. Put both hands together lightly, symbolizing unity, total confidence, right views, the pervasive Dharma nature, and the undiminished Buddha path.

### 33. What is the function of the BLIA Newsletter?

The BLIA Newsletter can serve the function of supporting members intellectually and emotionally, of providing information of events within the BLIA, and encouraging the practice of Buddhism.

### 34. How does one set up a new BLIA chapter?

Get a group together in someones house for teachings and practices. Ask guiding venerables, officers, or staff of the BLIA to meet with the group for clarification of the chapter's goals. Find new members and select staff members. Form a preparatory chapter.

### 35. How can someone develop a new subchapter of the BLIA?

Get together with local members, and invite the chairperson of a subchapter or a well-respected local citizen to form a preparatory subchapter. You can interpret the principles of the BLIA, nominate enthusiastic individuals as staff for the preparatory subchapter, sponsor Buddhist lectures, and invite trained persons to teach the Dharma.

### 36. How can one help a subchapter develop?

Hold staff training seminars and workshops, select outstanding members, support the subchapter in sponsoring activities, and promote regular temple visits. One can also encourage the subchapter to visit other branch temples, and to understand the operation of other subchapters in order to resolve any problems.

### 37. How can one establish a Buddha's Light community?

Allow BLIA members to take the initiative in developing community activities in the areas of culture, education, and public service. Earn the recognition of community members and further their willingness to join the BLIA through members' devotion to the Dharma and respect for the Triple Gem. Then, a Buddha's Light community, an ideal of a Pure Land in this world, can be achieved.

### 38. In what do BLIA staff members excel?

BLIA staff members excel in nurturing talents, in utilization of group wisdom and public experiences, in planning various meaningful and welcoming activities, and in carrying out charitable enterprises to benefit society. They also spread the supreme ideals of the BLIA to government institutions, schools, families, the community, and to every other facet of society.

## 39. How can one devise and sponsor training seminars for BLIA staff members?

Leadership training should be specific to each member's role within the organization. The content of every seminar should be consistent with the principles and spirit of the BLIA.

## 40. What activities should the BLIA sponsor?

Some examples are: Sports events, fairs, study groups, discussion groups, social services, disaster relief, protection of nature, environmental clean-up, music, dance, and movies.

## 41. What was the "Seven Admonitions Program"?

On October 17, 1993, when the BLIA sponsored the second All Member's General Meeting at the auditorium in Lin Kou, Taiwan, we established the "Seven Admonitions Program for purifying people's minds." The content included prohibitions against substance abuse, prostitution, violence, stealing, gambling, intoxication, and harsh words. We vowed to stop the perversions of drug use and prostitution, to promote Buddhist morality and ethics, and to establish the principles of a safe, joyous, and harmonious society.

## 42. What was the "Compassion and Love Program"?

Concerned about the safety of society, the BLIA initiated a "Compassion and Love Program" in May of 1997, in order to promote a movement in Taiwan to purify minds. The public response was favorable and extensive, and the BLIA initiated a ceremony where two thousand people took vows to be compassionate and loving. In addition, eighty thousand devotees, several Buddhist and other religious groups, and people from all walks of life, participated in this event. The BLIA expanded this event to every corner of the world, spreading compassion and loving kindness, endeavoring to promote the bright side of life.

### 43. What was the "Three Positive Solutions"?

Due to differences in values, materialism prevails and causes societal problems. On April 11, 1998, the BLIA began the "Three Positive Solutions" on the occasion of a Dharma function for welcoming the Buddha's tooth relic to Taiwan. In order to realize the good conditions of a virtuous life, the Three Positive Solutions movement proposes doing good things, for examples, transforming harmful actions into beneficial ethical deeds, speaking good words, and turning anger into praise, keeping good intentions, and changing ignorant minds into compassionate Bodhi minds.

### 44. What is the difference between the BLIA and other organizations?

The BLIA is an international organization whose participants are primarily Buddhists. The BLIA differs from other organizations in that members share a common religious belief. BLIA members not only seek spiritual liberation and wisdom, but also aim to create a peaceful, joyous society, and to enhance world peace.

### 45. Can others besides Buddhists join the BLIA?

The BLIA is a Buddhist organization that transcends geographic location, religion, and status. Buddhists who have taken refuge under the Triple Gem can join the BLIA and become members. As to those who believe in other religions but identify with the ideals of the BLIA, they can join and become "Friends of the BLIA."

### 46. How do members of the BLIA participate in activities sponsored by other temples?

Based on personal relationships, members of the BLIA can take part in the services or activities taking place at other temples. If more than three members of the BLIA wish to participate, they should attend as representatives of the BLIA by wearing the BLIA vests.

**47. What is the procedure if a subchapter wants to invite a venerable to give a talk?**

This is allowed if the invitation is to a monastic who is a member of the BLIA, but if a monastic non-member who is invited, permission must be granted by BLIA World Headquarters prior to giving the invitation.

**48. How do members of the BLIA acquire merit?**

They can voluntarily serve, give praise, and bestow blessings.

**49. How does the BLIA support the monastery?**

We advertise temple services and regular activities. We also assist with Dharma services, provided it does not conflict with BLIA activities. BLIA members participate in planning and preparation, receptions, advertisements, culinary tasks, serving meals, and directing traffic.

**50. What books are necessary for BLIA members?**

Books which members of the BLIA should read are: The Epoch of Buddha's Light, the Sutra on the Six Paramitas, the Agamas, the Diamond Sutra, Handing Down the Light, the Awakening of Faith in the Mahayana, the Platform Sutra of the Sixth Patriarch, the Lotus Sutra, the Diamond Sutra.

**51. What are the "Seven Wrong Actions" for members of the BLIA?**

Loaning money and goods, sexual misconduct, incorrect views, gossiping, spreading rumors, intervention in monastic affairs, and holding private services.

### 52. How do members of the BLIA associate with each other?

Members associate with each other by participation in public activities. Individual members shouldn't invite other members to private activities, thus avoiding problems among members. When weddings or funerals take place, the chairperson can invite other members to assist, provided time and distance are taken into consideration. Non-interference with a member's secular life should be used as a guideline.

### 53. How do members of the BLIA handle their financial affairs?

Members of the BLIA do not loan money to each other. If they start a business partnership, a legal contract should be created, and used as a guideline. Losses or gains should have nothing to do with the BLIA. Without permission from BLIA Headquarters, members of the BLIA cannot raise money on behalf of the organization.

### 54. How do members of the BLIA handle their feelings?

A. Improve feelings with compassion.

B. Purify feelings with supreme wisdom.

C. Classify feelings with etiquette.

D. Express feelings through ethics.

The BLIA encourages mutual admiration and affection between married couples, mutual respect and understanding between parents and offspring, and mutual appreciation among friends. When love and affection towards individuals can be transformed into a spirit of serving others, if self-centered possessiveness can be turned into brotherly love, and if affection for a few can be purified into universal benevolence toward every being, then all sentient beings will benefit.

# Stories about Venera...

$S$ince I became a monk, I have alw...
Buddhism and have tried to fulfill the idea ...
Land on earth. During the more than sixty year...
monk, there have been many touching stories in ...
story reflects my idea of practicing humanistic Buddh...
der to educate my disciples, devotees, and students, I will ...
examples below.

## Paying Extra for Shoes

In the summer of 1964, a man brought a big sack of Buddhist footwear to Shou Shan Temple where I was staying. He brought the shoes to sell to the monks in the temple, and I could see that he had worked hard to take them there. The weather had been very hot, and his back was soaked with sweat when he arrived. At the time we were quite poor. There were not very many monks in Taiwan in those days, and the business of selling us shoes couldn't have been all that profitable. When I asked him the price of a pair, he said, "One pair is 30 yuan." I took 40 yuan out of my pocket and gave it to him for a pair of shoes. He lifted his head and looked at me strangely when he saw that I was giving him an extra ten yuan. He said, "Everybody else always tries to bargain for a lower price, but you are giving me extra. Why is that?"

I said, "Selling shoes to monks is a tough business, but if you didn't do it, where would we get our shoes? If you can make a little extra, then you will stay in business and continue bringing us shoes. I'm not thinking only of you when I give you extra money, I'm also thinking of myself."

"I've never heard anyone say anything like that before, " he replied, rubbing the back of his head in mild wonderment.

e later, that same man sent his son to our temple to be-
monk.

## Auto Rest Home

In the 1960s, when there were still very few private automo-
biles being used in Taiwan, I decided to buy a car in order to help
us. In those days, people in Taiwan were still very traditional and
had a sort of prejudice towards monks and what they thought
monks should do, and should not do. A monk who wore a watch,
used a fountain pen or even rode a bicycle was suspect, and people
would talk about it critically. So, when I brought up the idea of
buying an automobile, many devotees were quite upset and op-
posed the plan. I didn't let them sway me, and the next day I went
to a car dealer.

At the dealer's, I discovered that if I bought a van instead of a
car, I would have to pay a little more, but we would be able to
carry many more people. Students and devotees then would be
able to travel with me as I spread the Dharma. I ended up buying a
van designed to seat nine people, but I got the car dealer to modify
it so it could carry as many as twenty-six people. The van had
small tires, and with the modifications made at the dealership, it
became very top-heavy, often and swaying and shaking as we
drove. Many times we went off the road and landed in ditches.
Once, we even flipped over! Thanks to the mercy of the Buddha,
no one got hurt, though we were shaken up a little that time.
Eventually, we got used to the van and people came to really enjoy it.

After about ten years, the van became pretty worn out. Many
devotees tried to persuade me to sell it and get a little money, but I
always refused to do so. At last, even some of the monks in the
temple began to think I was behaving strangely about the van by
keeping it around for no reason. I told them, "This old van has
been all over Taiwan with me. It's gone up and down practically

every street on the island. It has strained and worked all its life, and now that it's old and worn out, it can retire here. This can be its rest home."

## Sleep Punishment

When I first entered the monastic order as a boy, I was often forced to bow to the Buddha as punishment for not memorizing something correctly or for doing some other thing wrong. At the time, I remember thinking that bowing to the Buddha was a strange punishment because bowing to the Buddha was a good thing. It was something I loved to do.

Many years later, I established the Novice Training School for boys (ages 6-13) at Fo Guang Shan. The boys at the school were young and full of mischief, as boys are at that age. The teachers at the school fell in with tradition and started punishing the children by making them bow to the Buddha. When I found out about that, I said, "No, no, no. We don't do it that way here."

They replied, "If we don't make them bow, then how are we to punish them?"

I said, "Punish them by making them go to bed. *Don't* allow them to bow to the Buddha and *don't* allow them to join morning and evening chanting services."

They said, "But isn't that just exactly what they want? If we do that, won't we be rewarding them? Won't that make them even worse?"

I said, "I don't think so. Even though they'll be lying in their beds, they still will be able to hear the sounds of the other children chanting. With those sounds drifting into their ears, do you really think they will be able to sleep? When they see their classmates entering the hall for chanting, and they realize that they are not allowed to follow, they will understand that sleeping is a form of punishment and that bowing to the Buddha is a wonderful thing. They will naturally come to feel regretful about what they have done and want to change. When we are teaching people, we must first consider their emotions; then we can start to think about teaching them the Dharma. Above all, it is important that we respect them. With that as a foundation, we can begin to build their confidence and their image of themselves."

After using our new method of "sleep punishment" for half a year, the students at our school became quite self-controlled and good at monitoring their own behavior.

## A Little Dandelion

I've been teaching the Dharma for many years, and I've met with a lot of success and praise. I've also received many expensive and lavish gifts. But of everything I've ever been given, the gift that moved me the most was a little dandelion a little girl gave me one day in northwestern India.

A large crowd of people had gathered to say good-bye to us. People were everywhere. In the crowd, I caught a glimpse of a little girl holding a little dandelion. Her small lips were pursed as she shyly looked toward me. The good-bye ceremony ended, and at last we got in our car. Just as we were starting to drive away, the little girl with the dandelion raced up to us and pushed her little flower in between my window and the car door. I begged the driver to stop so I could give her a small string of prayer beads. As I gave her the beads, her face broke into the most beautiful smile. Then her little eyes brimmed and overflowed with tears.

As our car moved forward again, the yellow dandelion on the window gently shook in the breeze. In our rearview mirror, I could see the little girl still standing behind us. Her tiny body was straight and motionless. Her hands were pressed together before her in the traditional Indian gesture. As I watched her figure slowly grow smaller, my heart exploded with love.

## Taking Refuge Over the Phone

When we first started building Buddha's Light University, we raised money for the school by selling artwork that had been donated to us. Our efforts received a lot of public attention and many people helped us, so every time we had a sale, we were very successful. One day, Chen Xiao-Qun, who was in charge of publicity for these art sales, brought two of her friends by to see me. Her friends wanted to volunteer some of their time. As we talked together, the two said that they were amazed that we had been so successful in getting so many high quality works of art together for our sales. I took out a painting by Chang Da-Qian (a very famous 20th Century Chinese painter) called "Guan Yin Bodhisattva" to illustrate one way we acquired such paintings:

One evening, as the wind blew softly under a bright moon, I sat beside my window to read a stack of letters. One of the letters in the stack especially caught my attention. The letter was from someone named Gao Po Chen. Kao said his father, Gao Ling Mei, had taken ill and been sent to the hospital. Now that he was in the hospital, Ling-mei had expressed his wish to become a Buddhist. The Gaos lived in Hong Kong. At the end of his letter, Po Chen asked me if it would be possible for me to travel to Hong Kong to grant his father's wish? I was very touched that Po Chen wanted to help his father so much that he would send a letter like that to me.

It's a bit of a journey to go to Hong Kong from Taiwan, and, my schedule was already quite tight, I knew I would not be able to make the trip. I decided to do the refuge ceremony over the phone, instead. When we had finished with the ceremony, the entire Gao family was so grateful they decided to donate a painting to Fo Guang Shan. The painting turned out to be the one by Chang Da-Qian. As it turned out, Mr. Gao had been one of Hong Kong's most famous art collectors.

## Helping a Helper

I first discovered Qu Jia-Qun's talents as an editor through the work he did on a magazine directed toward young people who attended summer camps run by the government. Chu lived in Ilan so I asked him to help with the layout and editing of *Buddhism Today* and *Awakening the World* magazines. His work on those publications was excellent. His layouts were fresh and new, and his editorial decisions were very successful in drawing readers to us. His work was so creative he quickly became quite famous in magazine circles in Taiwan.

I still vividly remember Chu coming to Lei Yin Temple to do his work. I used to get everything ready for him. I laid out glue, scissors, pens, and paper on the table for him. I made sure that his pillow and blankets for his stayover had been freshly washed and ironed. I always folded them neatly and placed them on his bed.

Chu usually stayed up very late working. During that time I always hovered around him, assisting in any way I could. I used to bring him hot milk, noodles and other snacks to keep him going. He often protested, saying, "Master, it's late. Why don't you go to bed? I'll be all right by myself." No matter what he said, I always stayed with him until he was finished with his work. If the weather was cold, I would even give him my own blanket for the night.

Some of the people who knew what I was doing sometimes would ask me, "You are the master. Why do you treat one of your disciples as if you were his servant?"

I said, "He is putting so much energy into helping us to spread Buddhism, it is only right that I treat him with as much care and kindness as I can."

## A Resolution for 2/28

I first heard about the "2/28 Incident" when I came to Taiwan in 1949. (On February 28, 1947, thousands of Taiwanese were killed by the Kuomintang (KMT) government troops. The origins of the incident are unclear, but the "2/28 Incident" caused a long-lasting rift between native-born Taiwanese and immigrant Mainland Chinese, who made up the vast majority of KMT troops and officers. At the time, the KMT said the incident was an "in surrection," while most native-born Taiwanese considered it to be a massacre) The "2/28 Incident" was very disturbing to me, and I've tried my best to think of some way to lessen the pain and resentment caused by that tragedy.

In the early 1980s, I recommended that the government clear the names of those who had been killed in the incident. It wasn't until 1991, however, that conditions were suitable to do something to heal those old wounds. When the Chinese chapter of BLIA was established in Taiwan, we conducted a ceremony for those who had been killed in the incident. Both government officials and the families of those killed were present at the ceremony. Later, the remains of those who had been killed were interred in Fo Guang Shan's Wan Shou Cementery. Regular services still are held in their memory. I hope these efforts will be of some benefit in healing those old wounds and allowing people in Taiwan to move forward in a spirit of forgiveness and mutual acceptance.

In 1994, we hosted the "2/28 Memorial Music Concert" in Taipei. During a talk I gave at the concert, I suggested that everyone put the past behind them and move forward toward a community of peace and prosperity. After coming down from the stage, President Li Deng Hui, who happened to have a seat next to mine, complimented me on what I had said. He told me that my words had been very appropriate to the situation. The truth was, though, all I had done was to speak from my heart.

### Temple of the Universe

We were still in the middle of construction when Ni Ze-Zeng,

an engineer with the Taiwan Highway Bureau, first visited Fo
Guang Shan. Pilgrimage Hall had not yet been completed, and
there were signs of work going on in many other places on the hill.
We asked Ni Sze-tseng to stay with us for lunch. He said he
wanted to make a donation to the temple first. I told him there was
no need to do that. He looked a little uncomfortable because he
had always believed that he had to donate something every time
he ate at a temple. I said, "You are obviously so generous, Mr. Ni,
and I can see you really want to help us. Well then, please give us
a really big donation. Please pave the dirt road that leads to the
temple. That would be an enormous contribution to us and to the
local community. Our gratitude would know no bounds."

Mr. Ni replied, "I'll do it! I'll do it! Master, now I understand
that your monastery does not exist just for members of Fo Guang
Shan. You are building it for the whole universe. This is a Temple
of the Universe, here and everybody on earth should make a donation to you for building it!"

## Ice Capades

Twenty years ago, when I was Chancellor of Fo Guang Shan
Buddhist College, the Ice Capades were scheduled to come to
Kaohsiung to perform. The whole city was excited. One of our
students at the college, Liao Xiu Qi, became especially excited
about the prospect of seeing the Ice Capades.

"If I can't go to see them perform, I will regret it for the rest of
my life," she told one of her classmates. The problem was we had
a rule at our school that students were not allowed to leave campus
during times that classes were scheduled.

On the day of the performance, I asked Liao Xiu-Qi to come
to my office. I told her, "I want you to go to Kaohsiung and buy
some office supplies for us. There will be 300 yuan left over after
you have gotten everything. You can use that money for anything
you want, and it's OK if you return a little bit late. You don't need
to go ask any of your teachers for permission."

She laughed out loud, and smiling from ear to ear, said, "Thank you, thank you, Chancellor. I understand your meaning." After that day, she became one of our best students.

### Believing Versus Practicing Buddhism

Zao Cheng Chi is the founder of Taiwan's *Lifeline* suicide prevention hotline. His wife is a dedicated Buddhist. She converted to Buddhism over thirty years ago and has been an ardent practitioner of humanistic Buddhism ever since. When she first became a Buddhist, Mrs. Zao often spoke about Buddhism to her husband and encouraged him to come to the temple to chant sutras or to listen to talks. Since Mr. Zao did not believe in Buddhism, he found it difficult to deal with his wife's constant pushing. Even still, out of love for Mrs. Zao, he came to the temple with some regularity.

After one service at the temple, Mrs. Zao grabbed her husband's hand and pulled him over to me. She said, "Master, please help my husband increase his faith. Please teach him how to bow to the Buddha."

One look at the discomfort moving across Mr. Zao's face was enough to tell me to be careful with what I said. "Mr. Zao doesn't need to bow to the Buddha. All he needs to do is practice Buddhism in his daily life."

Mr. Zao was obviously well pleased with my reply, and afterwards he often told his friends, "Master Hsing Yun himself said I don't need to bow to the Buddha; I only need to practice Buddhism."

In the years since then, Mr. Zao has expended an immense amount of energy in helping others. He established Taiwan's *Lifeline*, frequently gives to the needy, started a scholarship fund for poor students, donated over ten thousand wheelchairs to the disabled and he has given large sums of money for disaster relief. Beyond all that, he also has committed himself to helping Hsi Lai Temple in Los Angeles, our temple in Paris and the BLIA.

Whenever someone compliments him on all the work he has done, Mr. Zao always answers, "Chanting the sutras is not as good as listening to them. Listening to the sutras is not as good as explaining them. Explaining the sutras is not as good as practicing what they say. I am just practicing Buddhism, that's all."

**Exercises:**

1. Give a brief description of your thoughts when reading this chapter.

2. Briefly describe the stories "Paying Extra for Shoes" and "Auto Rest Home" and give an explanation of what they taught you.

3. Do you think the stories "Sleep Punishment" and the "Ice Capades" reflect a proper way to provide an education?

## Chapter 19
## Stories about Devotees

*F*o Guang Shan promotes humanistic Buddhism, advocating the harmony of Buddhism and life. As members of the Buddha's Light, we should be in harmony with each other and respect each other, be united and tolerant, encourage and help each other, and be positive and diligent in order, to build a Pure Land on earth together. Today's Buddha's Light community is drawn from the many members of Buddha's Light organization who have contributed their efforts often without recognition. Their moving stories shine throughout the history of Fo Guang Shan. The following ten stories exemplify their compassionate contri- butions.

### A Gift of Two Legs

When Mrs. Chen Xu He took refuge, I gave her the Dharma name "Zu Che." Sometime later, while I was building the Kaohsuing Buddhist Hall, she traveled everywhere that her tiny feet would take her to raise the necessary funds. When the construction of Shou Shan temple began, I often saw her walking here and there, even though she had sore feet, seeking more donations to cover the building costs. Later, when we were building Fo Guang Shan, she still ran everywhere eagerly persuading people to donate. After the completion of the construction of Fo Guang Shan, I saw her volunteering in a retirement and nursing home. Whenever I saw her, I was so touched by her contributions and her attitude, and I always tried to offer her a few encouraging words.

When neighbors saw her working so diligently, they asked her, "Madam, Kaohsiung is such a big city. Why don't you take a bus? Besides you are not a monastic, why do you need to ask for contributions everywhere?""My master is so compassionate," she answered. "When he gave me the Dharma name 'Zu Che', he also gave me two legs (in Chinese, the character 'Che', 〔介〕, looks like two legs.) I want to use them to walk for my master!"There is no limit to the power of just one word!

## Behind the Scenes

When Fo Guang Shan was first being built, a young woman showed up one day. She was about twenty years old. When she saw what we were doing on the mountain, she made a vow to stay there and work in Kuole Restaurant, where we generated some of the funds used to support Da Zu Nursery School.

Whenever I passed by the restaurant, I always saw her smiling cheerfully as she prepared noodles for the customers. If there were only a few customers, she would still be just as cheerful as she straightened tables or did other small tasks, which were required. Even when the restaurant was very busy and packed with people, she always remained calm and helpful as she made sure that each person was well taken care of. From morning to night, day after day, she persisted in doing difficult, menial labor with an attitude of willingness and kindness all of us would do well to emulate.

I have watched her for over thirty years, as her dark black hair has slowly turned to grey. Out of respect and admiration for her contributions to Buddhism, I have provided her with living quarters at Fo Guang Shan. Her name is Guo Dao-Guang.

Da Zu Nursery School frequently wins prizes for excellence, and we often are complimented on the good work we do. Whenever people speak to me about how excellent the school is, I can never help but think of people like Kuo Tao-kuang, who selflessly and tirelessly worked for years only to benefit others.

And I wonder, how many of us are really sufficiently appreciative of all the people in the world like her who have contributed so much to our continuing growth and development? Where would any of us be without them?

## This Is My Home

During the Sino-Japanese War, Tai Bao Cheng became deaf in both ears. After coming to Taiwan, he started working at Shou Shan Temple. Later, when Fo Guang Shan was established, Tai became a cook in the restaurant located in Pilgrimage Hall. He worked there peacefully and quietly for twenty years.

Since he could hear nothing at all, Tai was forced to pay extra attention to the small details of the kitchen. One of the most difficult jobs in the kitchen was to determine how much food was needed on any given day. It was always difficult to predict how many people would arrive, or how many might suddenly leave. With his sharp eye for the world around him and his attentiveness to detail, Tai became very good at estimating how much rice to make and how many vegetables to prepare. Tai was never moody or involved in any sort of conflict with anyone. Even if he were not feeling well, he still would show up for work and do his job to the best of his ability.

After travel between Taiwan and Mainland China was permitted in 1987, Tai's supervisor thought it would be appropriate to offer to pay Tai's travel expenses back to his original home for a visit. When he told Tai what he had decided, Tai replied simply, "Go back to what home? *This* is my home. I have nowhere else to go."

Tai's supervisor accepted his refusal, but upon hearing what the reasons was, he immediately arranged for Tai to be given lodgings at Fo Guang Shan for the rest of his life.

## Inner Engines

Yu Ze Lang was a salesman for a manufacturer of engines and machines in Jiayi, Taiwan. Yu was also an active member of the local branch of the BLIA.

Yu worked diligently for Buddhism all year long. But each year, just before Chinese New Year, Yu would work even more. Several days before the New Year, Yu would always come with a couple of his friends to Fo Guang Shan to set up the thousands of "Peace Lanterns" we used to celebrate the occasion.

Coincidentally, the end of the year was also the easiest time to sell engines. People often asked him, "Why do you always come to Fo Guang Shan just when business is best? What benefit can that give you?"

Yu always would answer with great seriousness, "When people come here and see the lanterns and venerate the Buddha, they feel renewed and are willing to continue with life in a positive manner. I may not be selling engines in town, but by being here I am restarting the engines in people's hearts."

I've watched Yu for years. He's always smiling, friendly, and considerate of others. Yu has not only started the engine in his own heart, he has lighted the brilliant lamp of Buddhism, as well.

## Lotus Gesture

One summer while Chen Jun Yi was on a trip, he had a short layover in Thailand. While he was waiting in the airport, Chen had his wallet stolen by a pickpocket. His passport and airline ticket were still safe in another pocket, but all of his money had been taken.

Chen became nervous when he realized that he had no way to pay his airport tax, or to take care of any other necessity that might suddenly arise. Then he had a moment of inspiration: Chen remembered that he was a BLIA member and that the BLIA was an international organization. Wouldn't there be a chance that some member of the BLIA would pass through the airport in the next hour or so?

Chen thought there would be, so he decided to stand outside in front of the main doors of the airport, where he could greet everyone who came in with the lotus gesture of the BLIA. His idea worked rather quickly. After only a few minutes, a member of the BLIA, who was in Thailand on a business trip, noticed Chen and came over to him.

The two of them were pleased to meet each other, and when the man heard about Chen's problem, he was even more pleased to extend the hand of friendship by lending Chen enough money to pay his airport tax and meet any unexpected needs.

From that point on, Chen's return flight to Taiwan was a breeze. Today, Chen still enjoys telling the story of the lotus gesture and the pleasure of finding a helping hand just when he needed one the most.

### A Late Guest

Darkness had fallen. Stars flickered in the sky. Evening chanting services already had ended. The incense master had thrown the bolt across the great door of Buddha Hall.

He walked a few steps away from the large doors when he saw an old woman running up the stairs toward him. She was gasping with great effort when she spoke, "Master! Master! Wait a moment! I want to make a donation."

"The hall is closed for the night. I'm sorry. Can you come again tomorrow?"

As the incense master was speaking, the abbot of the temple, Xin Ting, drew near enough to hear the woman's reply.

"I'm sorry," she said, "but I've come all the way from Hualien. It took me all day to get here. I couldn't help but be late. Today is the day I promised the Buddha I would make a donation to the temple. I've been selling old newspapers for a year to save money to make this donation. Please let me go inside! I promised I would make the donation today!"

When Xin Ting heard what the woman had to say, he immediately stepped forward to greet her very cordially. Then he asked the incense master to open the Buddha Hall so the woman could go in. Xin Ting then waited until she was finished. When the woman came out, Xin Ting personally escorted her to Pilgrimage Hall where he helped her register for the night.

The next morning, when it was time for the woman to leave, she stood for a long time gazing at a golden statue of the Buddha, tears slowly running from her eyes. A nun standing beside her heard her say, "In my whole life I have never been treated this well by anyone."

## The Farmer of Culture and Education

Twenty years ago, Taiwan's Buddhists understood the importance of helping the poor and the weak, and donating for publishing books and dedicating of Buddhist statues. At the same time, there were also some people who understood the importance of culture and education. For example, there was Mr. Chen Shun Quan, the advisor of BLIA, Tainan. From an early time, he had always donated money for Buddhist culture and education. He provided scholarships for Fo Guang Shan Buddhist college students, offered funds for the editing of the Tripitaka, and gave money to the Fo Guang Shan Foundation Fund for Culture and Education. Mr. Chen was always eager to do these things.

People asked him, "Why do you donate money for culture and education? Do you do this because you feel that it is a meritorious deed?"

He replied, "I never think about whether or not I am performing a meritorious deed. I only think about how Buddhist culture and education is like plowing a piece of the field of good merits."

Even today, Mr. Chen calls himself "an old farmer planting seeds in the field of culture and education."

## Unmarried His Whole Life

One day, as Mr. Yen Wei Kung drove south to join a pilgrimage to Fo Guang Shan, he suddenly became caught in a traffic jam at Shan I. As he listened to local reports about the traffic situation on his car radio, Mr. Yen learned that very close to where he was, there was a serious car accident. More than ten cars had crashed. Without hesitation, carrying his medical emergency kit, he got out of his car to do what he could to be part of the rescue work.

The situation was a mess. All around were mangled cars. Smoke filled the air as rescue workers labored to take care of the accident victims. While he worked to move some of the injured, Mr. Yen heard the sound of a baby crying. In the midst of all of the confusion he also heard a sigh. Following the voice, he walked toward a blue car that had been badly smashed and was lying upside down. A weak voice called out to him, "Sir, here...I beg you...."

Mr. Yen kneeled down and saw that the man in the front seat was dead. In the back seat, a young woman's face was bleeding. Showing him the baby in her arms, she said weakly, "I am dying...help my little girl...." Those were her last words. The young mother closed her eyes and stopped breathing.

Ten years later, that same little girl was a fourth grade student in an elementary school. She also has a very warm family. However, something is missing. This family has no female householder. Mr. Yen was afraid that if he got married, his wife might not treat this little girl kindly. So, even though many people have tried to introduce him to various single women, he has always rejected the notion. Whenever his friends have tried to persuade him, he has always replied, "In a previous life, the Buddha sacrificed himself to save a pigeon. He also cut off some of his flesh to feed an eagle. My little sacrifice is nothing when compared to that of the Buddha!"

## A Promise

After Liao Jui-fu moved to Taipei, he became a regular participant in Pu Men Temple's Friday night Chan meditation sessions. A few years after that, Liao retired and started coming to the temple every day to help in one way or another.

A person who frequently volunteers to work at a Buddhist temple sometimes is called a "Guardian of the Temple." After Liao became a "Guardian of Pu Men Temple," his friends began to wonder what had happened to him because they rarely saw him anymore. Liao explained to everyone, "I have two homes now. One is my regular home that all of you know, and the other is Pu Men Temple where I spend almost as much time."

Liao's life went on like that for nine more years until he decided to move to Canada to be with his children. Just before he left Taiwan, Liao arranged to have a retired old soldier come to take his place at the temple every day. Liao paid the soldier a good wage to come every day for a full year to take over his duties.

When the nuns at the temple heard what he had arranged, they told him, "Mr. Liao, we are very grateful that you are so concerned about the temple, but there is no need to hire someone to come work in your place! Pu Men Temple has many guardians who will be able to fill in for you. You should just relax and enjoy your move to Canada."

When he heard them say this, Liao's face became perfectly still and even seriousness.

"No, I can't do that," he said. "Years ago I vowed before the Buddha that I would work here as a guardian for ten years. There is still one year left in that vow. I would never be contented in Canada if I left here without fulfilling my vow."

## Earning Joy

Thirty years ago, while we were building Shou Shan Temple, Hsiao Ting-hsun was an ordinary worker. I noticed, however, that even though Hsiao had had no special training, he was really very talented when it came to construction. Some years later when we were ready to start constructing Fo Guang Shan, I remembered Hsiao, and I asked him to come and oversee the project.

I can still recall those early days very well. We planned our work pretty much without using any blueprints. We measured things with a tape measure, and used stones to draw our plans in the dirt. As we drew, we discussed how we wanted things to look. The two of us talking together in the shade on a warm afternoon was pretty much the way all of Fo Guang Shan was created. We were often short of money in those days, but I always did my best to be sure Hsiao had enough to pay his workers. I often asked him if he needed more.

Over the years, communication between the two of us became so easy, we hardly needed to talk anymore. I knew what he needed to get a job done, and he was capable of comprehending what I wanted almost before I spoke.

Thirty years passed quickly. Hsiao's children, and finally even his grandchildren, came to Fo Guang Shan to help us with construction. Sometimes Hsiao would say quite proudly to people, "I'm the guy who built Fo Guang Shan."

Over the years, many construction companies tried to take Hsiao away from us. They offered him very high wages, but Hsiao always refused to work for anyone else. If people ever asked him why he had given his life to a cause that paid him so little, Hsiao would usually answer, "I work here not to earn money, but to earn joy. There is no material pleasure in the world that can compare to the joy of doing something of value to others."

**Exercises:**

1. Describe the story that impressed you the most and how you feel about it.

2. Describe any inspiration you received from these stories of compassion.

3. List two examples of compassion in these stories.

# Chapter 20
# The Important Events in Fo Guang Shan's History

*W*hen Fo Guang Shan celebrated its 30th anniversary and decided to close the monastery to visitors, we carved the important events of the past 30 years on a wall in front of the Tathagata Hall. Here is an overview of the main events of Fo Guang Shan's history, year by year.

### 1967— 1st year of Buddha's Light
**May:** Venerable Master Hsing Yun purchased 30 acres of bamboo forest in Kaohsiung, Da Xu County for construction. That same year on May 16th, the groundbreaking ceremony and the official naming of Fo Guang Shan took place. At that time, the four objectives of Fo Guang Shan were established; "To propagate Buddhism through culture, to train talent through education, to benefit society through charity work, and to purify peoples' minds through practice."

**July:** Fo Guang Shan Buddhist Order acquired Lan Yang Christian Mission in Ilan and changed the name to Ren Ai Chi Jia. We attended to more than a hundred elderly and poor. We also established Buddha's Light Vihara and Da Zu Nursery School at Fo Guang Shan.

### 1968— 2nd year of Buddha's Light
**December:** The construction of Fo Guang Shan Buddhist College began. Wu Xiu-Qi, Pan Xia-Rue, along with 28 benefactors, donated the classrooms. Wu Da Hai (great ocean) donated the water tower and we named it "water of the great ocean."

### 1969— 3rd year of Buddha's Light

**March**-Tzu Hui, Tzu Jia and Tzu Yi went to Japan for further study. They studied in Kyoto, at Ohtani Buddhist University. They were the first group of Fo Guang Shan monastics to study abroad. Later on Venerables Tzu Chuang, Tzu Jung, Yi Jie, Yi Kung, Yi Yu, Yi En, Yi Hua, Huei Kai, Yi Fa, Yi Yi, Yung Yu, Yung Chi, Man Ding, Chueh Cheng, Miao Qing, and others studied in Japan, Korea, India, USA, England, and Brazil. Now they all have Masters and Ph.D. degrees.

**July:** The first Buddhist summer camp for college students was held, with students coming from 26 Taiwanese universities. More than a hundred young people joined Xue Cheng Chi, Shen Ren Yi, and Chao Zui Hui. This was an important event in Buddhist history.

### 1970—4th year of Buddha's Light

**December:**--The inauguration of Da Zu Nursery School. Venerables Tzu Jung, Tzu Jia, Tzu Yi, Yi Jie, and Yi Lai were a few of the past presidents. This nursery school takes care of orphans from all over the world.

### 1971—5th year of Buddha's Light

**April:** The Great Compassion Shrine was completed. It was the first hall at Fo Guang Shan. Over 100,000 people attended the opening ceremony, including the head of the Ministry of the Interior, Xu Qing Zhong, who presided over the ribbon cutting.

### 1972—6th year of Buddha's Light

**May:** The president of Singapore, Mr. Li Guang Yao, and his wife visited Fo Guang Shan.

### 1973—7th year of Buddha's Light

**June:** The President of the Executive Yuan, Jiang Qing Guo, visited Fo Guang Shan and praised the achievements in construction, culture, and education. In 1976 he visited Fo Guang Shan for the third time to see the construction site of the welcoming Buddha. In 1978, the day after being elected president of the Republic of China, he visited the main Buddha Hall to pay respects and praise the contribution of Fo Guang Shan in teaching Buddhism in the modern world.

### 1974—8th year of Buddha's Light

**April:** Venerable Master Hsing Yun was appointed as the president of the Association of Sino-Japanese Buddhists. To promote these cultural relations, he visited Japan. The next year, he again led a group to visit Japan and Korea. In Seoul, he established the Chinese-Korean Buddhist Association to promote positive relations.

**August:** The president of the Japanese-Chinese Buddhist Association, Niwa Renho, visited Fo Guang Shan again in 1977.

### 1975—9th year of Buddha's Light

**March:** Ven. Tzu Hui became the publisher of *Awakening the World* magazine, which was produced in 1957. This magazine introduces humanistic Buddhism to Fo Guang Shan devotees. In 1995 this magazine changed from being published every ten days to being published once a month. The circulation has reached 400,000 copies.

**May:** Groundbreaking started at Fu Shan Temple in Chang Hua. Ven. Hsin Ping was responsible for that construction. It was Fo Guang Shan's first branch temple.

**October:** Venerable Master Hsing Yun conducted a three-day series of talks at the National Arts Hall. It was the first time that a Buddhist lecture was held in one of the halls of government.

### 1976—10th year of Buddha's Light

**March:** Published the first issue of Buddha's Light Scholarly

Journal. It was the beginning of our Buddhist academic research.

**July:** Venerable Master Hsing Yun led a group of Chinese Buddhists on a visit to America in order to participate in its 200th anniversary. At that time, he decided to establish a temple in the United States.

### 1977—11th year of Buddha's Light

**July:** The opening ceremony of Fo Guang Shan, Pu Men High School was held. Ven. Tzu Hui was appointed the first president. The Buddha's Light Tripitaka editing committee was established for re-editing using a more modern way of punctuation, paragraph arrangement, commentary and footnotes. This more modern structure and phraseology is used to increase reader interest.

**November:** The first time the Ten Thousand Buddhas Triple Platform Ordination was held. It has become the model for similar ceremonies.

### 1978—12th year of Buddha's Light

**March:** Established Taipei branch temple on Song Jiang Road was established. Ven. Tzu Zhuang became the abbess.

The institute of Chinese Buddhist research opened classes in Taipei.

Mr. Chang Da-Qian and his wife visited Fo Guang Shan to present his painting of "One Flower, One World."

**August:** Venerable Master Hsing Yun was awarded an honorary Ph.D. from the University of Oriental Studies in Los Angeles, USA. He also held the groundbreaking ceremony for Hsi Lai Temple in Los Angeles.

### 1979—13th year of Buddha's Light

**January:** This was the first time a Buddhist concert was held in Taipei's Sun Yat-sen Memorial Hall (or any national facility).

**August:** The first time Fo Guang Shan developed a children's Buddhist summer camp. Three thousand people participated. Now a youth winter camp, mother's summer camp, and a teacher's summer camp are held annually. Taiwan television started the program "Sweet Dew" (Gan Lu). It was the first example of Buddhist teaching on TV. The show was given the social education Golden Bell Award by the Ministry of Education and the Government Information Office.

**October:** *Universal Gate* magazine was launched.

## 1980—14th year of Buddha's Light

**April:** Venerable Master Hsing Yun wrote the words to "Ode to the Triple Gem," and the "Song of Fo Guang Shan." Professor Wu Zhu Che wrote the music.

**May:** Venerable Master Hsing Yun became the director of the Chinese Cultural University's Indian Research Institute. It was the first Buddhist institute approved by the Ministry of Education to award degrees.

## 1981—15th year of Buddha's Light

**March:** The President of Dong Hai University, Mei Ko Wang, invites Venerable Master Hsing Yun to teach a philosophy course.

**December:** The 15th anniversary of Fo Guang Shan was observed with the inauguration of the Main Buddha Hall. All senior monastics returned for the ceremony. One hundred thousand people joined the ceremony, including representatives from the USA, France, Korea, and Japan.

## 1982—16th year of Buddha's Light

**October:** The writer, Alexander Solzhenitsyn, visited Fo Guang Shan.

**December:** Fo Guang Shan became "brother" temple with Tongdosa in Korea. The ceremony was held in the Kaohsiung Cultural Center.

## 1983—17th year of Buddha's Light

**September**: Ven. Tzu Yi was put in charge of the Agama Tripi-taka collection. A chronology of Buddhist history was published in 1987.

### 1984—18th year of Buddha's Light

**July:** We established a mobile clinic to offer free medical care to those in need in remote areas of Taiwan. This provided an opportunity for those who are more fortunate to help the poor in getting medical attention. Later on we purchased a medical van from Japan and established Yun Shui Hospital.

**September:** Venerable Master Hsing Yun established the first Buddhist City College in Kaohsiung, providing an opportunity for everyone to learn Buddhism.

### 1985—19th year of Buddha's Light

**September:** Master Hsing Yun transmitted the Dharma and passed the abbotship of Fo Guang Shan over to Ven. Hsin Ping. From then on, following the Buddhist system, the Dharma was transmitted to management through a system of leadership, which set an example for monastery democracy.

### 1986—20th year of Buddha's Light

**December:** The World Sutric and Tantric Buddhist Confer-ence was held at Fo Guang Shan. The leaders of the four schools of Tantric Buddhism attended the conference.

Venerables Tzu Jung, Hui Lung, Yi Jung, Xiao Chueh, and now Yung Sheng were awarded the National Good People, Good Events Award by the Ministry of the Interior.

### 1987—21st year of Buddha's Light

**May:** Venerable Master Hsing Yun met the President of the Chinese Buddhist Association, Zhao Puchu, in Bangkok, Thai-land. Their conversation was very positive.

**July:** Venerable Master Hsing Yun invited 1200 people to celebrate their 60th birthdays at Fo Guang Shan.

## 1988—22nd year of Buddha's Light

**February:** The Mayor of Alhambra, California, Peng Ko, presented Master Hsing Yun with the Honorable Citizen Award along with the keys to the city.

**June:** Fo Guang Shan celebrated its 20th anniversary. It also held the first alms-round fundraising event for the Fo Guang Shan Cultural and Educational Foundation. Ven. Tzu Hui was appointed president of the foundation in order to promote cultural and educational professions.

**August:** The first time a short-term monastic retreat was held. Eight thousand people registered, although only one thousand people were approved. In order to accommodate so many people, they were separated into three groups, which were scheduled to attend at different times.

**October:** The Taiwan Government Information Office honored the publisher of the Buddha's Light Encyclopedia. The following year another award was received from the R.O.C. Ven. Zu Yi and a committee of nine took more than ten years to complete the project. Venerables Tzu Chuang, Tzu Hui, Tzu Jung, Tzu Jia, Tzu Yi, Yi Yen, Yi Kung, Yi Zun, Da He, Yung Xiang, Chueh Ming, and 100 other workers cooperated to complete the project.

**November:** The sixteenth conference of the World Fellowship of Buddhists was held at Hsi Lai Temple. It was the first time the meeting was held in this region. It was also the first time for an equal exchange between the People's Republic of China and the Republic of China.

**November:** The opening ceremony of Hsi Lai Temple was held on 26th. It was acknowledged as the biggest Buddhist temple in North America. Ven. Tzu Chuang was appointed the first abbess. The Triple Platform Ordination Ceremony was held at Hsi

Lai Temple. Monastics came from 16 countries, and 300 candidates were ordained.

## 1989—23rd year of Buddha's Light

**January:** The International Chan conference was held at Fo Guang Shan. Representatives came from China, the United States, Korea, Japan, Hong Kong, and Italy. More than 50 scholars from the East and West presented their papers. Among the participants were Lewis Lancaster, Ph.D., and John McRae, Ph.D., from the United States, Professor Santina from Italy, Nakamura Hajime, Mizuno Kougen and Hirakawa Akira from Japan, and Kim Young Doo from Korea. Cheng Shih-yen represented Taiwan and Yang Tseng-wen represented China.

**January:** Venerable Master Hsing Yun was invited by the State legislature of California to hold a purification ceremony. This was the first time that a Buddhist ceremony was held in this government facility. Later on in New York and San Diego the City Councils invited monastics from our order to perform opening ceremonies.

**January:** United States Senator Al Gore visited Fo Guang Shan. In April of 1996 Vice-President Al Gore visited Hsi Lai Temple, USA.

**March:** President Zhao Puchu of the Chinese Buddhist Association invited Venerable Master Hsing Yun to lead 200 monastics and lay people for a one-month visit to Mainland China in order to visit his hometown.

**July:** The spiritual leader of Tibet, His Holiness the Dalai Lama, visited Hsi Lai Temple, USA.

**November:** Since 1983's establishment of the Fo Xiang Vihara in Hong Kong, Venerable Master Hsing Yun has given several talks there to promote Buddhism.

**December:** The first meeting of Fo Guang Shan benefactors was held to pass bylaws and develop methods of promotion. To improve the harmony of the monastic and lay followers,

Venerable Master Hsing Yun proposed that all honor go to the Buddha, achievements to the majority, benefits to the temples, and merits to the benefactors.

### 1990—24th year of Buddha's Light

**February:** Fo Guang Shan Religions Affairs Committee held its second membership conference electing Venerables Hsin Ping, Tzu Chuang, Tzu Hui, Tzu Jung, Tzu Jia, Tzu Yi, Hsin Ting, Yi Hung, and Yi Kung as committee members to establish bylaws and an organizational system.

**July:** Hsi Lai University in the United States registered with the California Department of Education in order to grant degrees to students.

**November:** Fo Guang Shan Cultural Education Fund Foundation held The World Buddhist Examination. One million two hundred thousand people from Taiwan, Hong Kong, Australia, Asia, and the Americas participated in the examination.

### 1991—25th year of Buddha's Light

**February:** The International Buddhist Association, Republic of China, held its opening ceremony at Sun Yat-sen Memorial Hall on February 3rd. Venerable Master Hsing Yun was appointed president and Ven. Tzu Jung was appointed general secretary.

**February:** The Republic of China chapter of the BLIA held a ceremony to comfort victims of the February 28th tragedy.

**March:** *Hsing Yun's Dharma Words* was broadcast on Taiwan television. The news department gave the show the Golden Bell Award. In 1994 they broadcast *Hsing Yun's Sayings*. Taiwan television broadcast *Hsing Yun's Parables*. From then on the three TV stations have broadcast Buddhist teaching programs daily.

**March:** The head of the Bronkhorstspruit City Council of South Africa, Dr. Hennie Senekal, visited Fo Guang Shan and invited Fo Guang Shan to go to South Africa to build a temple. Venerable Hui Lee was put in charge of the project.

**September:** Fo Guang Shan established a branch temple in a chateau outside Paris and began to spread the Dharma in Europe. In the following year BLIA chapters were established in England, Germany, France, and Switzerland.

### 1992—26th year of Buddha's Light

**March:** The Buddha's Light Pure Land Cultural Education Fund Foundation was established. Venerable Tzu Chuang was put in charge with the purpose of establishing branch temples around the world.

**May:** More than 4,000 people attended the first meeting of the Los Angeles, BLIA, which was held at the Los Angeles Music Center. This meeting's theme was to promote the "joy and harmony." Venerable Master Hsing Yun was elected president. The mayor of Monterey Park, Mr. Jiang Guo Liang, announced that May 16th would be the day of Buddha's Light.

**July:** Devotee Chang Sheng-Kai donated his residence for the establishment of Ru Lai Temple, the first branch temple in Sao Paolo, Brazil, South America. Venerables Chueh Cheng and Chueh Sheng were put in charge.

**September:** The mayors of the cities of Austin and Houston, Texas presented their Honorary Citizenship Award to Venerable Master Hsing Yun.

**October:** Fo Guang Shan organized The World Buddhist Fellowship Association, with the opening ceremony held in Taipei at Yang Min Shan, Zhung Shan building. Venerable Master Hsing Yun was appointed as permanent honorary president of the World Buddhist Fellowship Association.

**October:** Ven. Yung Chuan oversaw construction of Zhung Tian Temple in Brisbane, Australia. After its completion, Ven. Yi Lai was appointed abbess.

**November:** The Ministry of Education of the Republic of

China recognized the BLIA organization for making great contributions to social education. The General Secretary of the BLIA, Ven. Tzu Rong, accepted the award and arrangements were made to meet President Lee Deng Hui. The BLIA also received this award the following three years.

**November:** Fo Guang Shan's Cultural Education Fund Foundation, which has promoted the purification of people's minds, was presented the second Harmony of Society Award for outstanding promotion of social order. President Lee Deng Hui presented the award.to Ven. Tzu Hui.

### 1993—27th year of Buddha's Light

**February:** A Buddha's Light meeting held at Fo Guang Shan for the parents and families of the monastic disciples.

**October:** BLIA held the first International Buddhist Sangha Seminar to promote exchange and cooperation among international Buddhist groups. Monastics and lay people from 16 countries participated. The second and third seminars were held in Vancouver, Canada and Sydney, Australia. More than 60 representatives from as far as the United States, Australia, and England attended.

**October:** The 2nd annual BLIA conference was held at Fo Guang Shan. Thirty thousand attended the opening ceremony in Lin Go Coliseum, Tao Yuan County. President Lee Deng Hui attended. At the meeting Santiago Ruperez, director of the Spanish Chamber of Commerce, took refuge along with five South Africans.

**October:** The Ministry of Education of the Republic of China approved the establishment of Buddha's Light University. Ven. Tzu Hui was given the responsibility for fund raising. Mr. Gong Peng Cheng was appointed president of Nan Hua Management College in Chia Yi County.

**October:** Venerable Master Hsing Yun initiated the Purification of People's Minds Movement. The Seven Commandants, which include: no use of cigarettes, drugs, violence, greed, alcohol, sexual misconduct, gambling, and harsh speech, were described.

### 1994—28th year of Buddha's Light

**February:** Taipei Temple was formally inaugurated on the Chinese New Year. Ven. Tzu Jung was appointed as the first abbess.

**October:** Ten African students were ordained in Nan Hua Temple in South Africa. They were the first group of Africans in history to be ordained. It was a big step toward introducing Buddhism to South Africa.

**December:** The Fo Guang Tripitaka Editing Committee published a 51-volume collection of the Chan canon. The committee headed by Venerables Yung Ming and Yung Chin, and a staff of over ten people. The following year, the Fo Guang Shan Cultural Education Fund Foundation donated 1,000 copies of this Chan Canon to universities, libraries, and temples.

### 1995-29th year of Buddha's Light

**January:** *Handing Down the Light*, the biography of Venerable Master Hsing Yun, was published by Commonwealth Publishing Company and was a top seller in Kingstone Bookstores; The author of *Handing Down the Light,* Fu Chi Ying, was awarded the top honor for female writers in Taiwan.

**February:** At a Buddhist meeting in India, more than one hundred thousand members awarded Venerable Master Hsing Yun the Buddha's Gem Award.

**April:** On April 7th, Ven. Hsin Ping passed away. Religious Affairs Committee elected Ven. Hsin Ting to serve as the sixth abbot of Fo Guang Shan.

**April:** On April 25th, Venerable Master Hsing Yun had heart surgery in Taipei at Jong Min Veterans Hospital. Dr. Zhang Yen was in charge of the operation.

**July:** The International Exchange Meeting of Catholics and Buddhists held its opening ceremony at Ru Lai Hall. Ven. Hsin Ting presided over the meeting. Cardinal Francis Arinze was invited to give a talk. More than 2,000 people joined the ceremony.

**September:** The Fo Guang Shan 10-volume series on Buddhism was published and presented to monastics, Shi Gu's, lay Dharma teachers, and benefactors to provide them with a tool for both teaching and self-study.

### 1996—30th year of Buddha's Light

**April:** Malaysia BLIA chapter, and the Malaysia Buddhist Association invited Venerable Master Hsing Yun to give a talk at Salaam Stadium. He spoke about the compassion of humanistic Buddhism. 80,000 people attended.

**May:** A 100-volume collection of Chinese Buddhist Sutras was published. The work on this collection was the responsibility of Chi Guang Yu and Venerables Man Qi and Yung Ying. This collection presents Buddhist sutras in a modern and more readable format. The "100 religious Question Series" was published next.

**September:** Supervised by the Fo Guang Shan Religious Affairs Committee, the Buddha's Light Dictionary CD (preliminary test version) was finished.

**September:** This was the first showing of the Fo Guang Shan 30th Anniversary Memorial Film. The president of the Central Film Company, Qiu Xun Qing, and director Wang Dong presided over the ceremony.

**September:** Buddha's Light University, Nan Hua College held its grand opening ceremony. This is the first university in Taiwan to not charge a tuition fee. More than 10,000 people attended the celebration.

**October:** The 30th anniversary of Fo Guang Shan was celebrated. The first World Buddhist Outstanding Women's Conference was also held at Fo Guang Shan. More than 500 outstanding women, coming from 15 different countries, attended this four-day conference.

The achievements and accomplishments over the 30-year history of Fo Guang Shan have increased the confidence of the devotees, purified society, and improved the social order. We have established more than 100 branch temples that allow us to teach the Dharma and benefit sentient beings in many parts of the world. At this stage we can say we have accomplished our goals by working through religious functions to benefit others and to help society. With one step, we have left one footprint and we have written a permanent chapter in Buddhist history.

### 1997—31st year of Buddha's Light

**January:** A five-day International Buddhist Youth Conference was held. More than 600 Buddhist young people, coming from 20 countries, joined the meeting. Well-known writer from Mainland China, Yu Chou Yue, was invited to give a talk.

**February:** Venerable Master Hsing Yun visited the Vatican in Rome, Italy to participate in a dialogue with Pope John Paul II in order to encourage religious exchange and pray for world peace.

**March:** The spiritual leader of Tibet, His Holiness the Dalai Lama, was invited to Taiwan to visit Fo Guang Shan. Ven. Hsin Ting and His Holiness the Dalai Lama led the gathering in the main Buddha hall. Prayers and chanting by 5,000 monastics and lay people were conducted in both the Chinese and Tibetan languages. His Holiness gave a talk in the auditorium after which he was presented with the Chan Buddhist Canon.

**May:** Fo Guang Shan Religious Affairs Committee held the Closing of the Mountain ceremony and the ceremony for the sixth abbot of Fo Guang Shan, Ven. Hsin Ting.

Venerable Master Hsing Yun received an award from the Ministry of the Interior and the Taiwan Ministry of Foreign Affairs.

A Love and Compassion Program was organized in the south and north of Taiwan. There were 80,000 people that participated in the Taipei Campaign.

The Buddha's Light Tripitaka Prajna Canon was published. There are a total of 42 volumes.

The first Fo Guang Shan electronic dictionary-in compact disc format was published.

**November:** Venerable Hsin Ting received an award from the Taiwan Ministry of Education.

**December:** Venerable Master Hsing Yun received the First Class Award from the Kuomintang political party.

The Buddha's Light TV station held their opening ceremony at Ling Ko Coliseum. Programming commenced in January 1998.

## 1998—32nd year of Buddha's Light

**January:** To promote positive interaction among Buddhist temples, the first Taiwan Buddhist Temples Administration seminar was held. The second, third and fourth seminars, were held in April and December of 1998, and April of 1999, respectively.

**February:** The Vice President of the Republic of China, Lian Chen, along with the Advisor to President Wu Poh-Hsiung, Xu Li De, visited Fo Guang Shan. The Vice President presented a plaque "Great Compassionate Love" to Fo Guang Shan.

To re-establish the Bhikshuni Lineage in the Theravada tradition, the International Triple Platform performed an ordination ceremony, which was held in Bodhgaya, India. Over 150 novitiates from more that 20 countries, came to participate. It was the first time that China held an ordination ceremony in India.

Ten volumes of "Buddhism," edited by Venerable Master Hsing Yun, were published.

**March:** Fo Guang Shan's English name was formally abbreviated to FGS, by a meeting of Fo Guang Shan's committee of Religious Affairs. Fo Guang Shan, at the request of devotees, was opened for weekend practice.

**April:** The Buddha's Tooth relic was delivered to Taiwan. The Welcome for the Buddha's Tooth Ceremony was held at Chung Cheng Memorial Hall.

**December:** The Buddha's Tooth relic was carried to Kaohsiung from Taipei by train and is awaiting the completion of the Buddha's Tooth Memorial Temple to be completed so that it can be put on display.

102-year-old Sri Lankan Grand Master, Ven. Ananda Maitraya Maha Nayaka, led a group to visit Fo Guang Shan.

**May:** Venerable Master Hsing Yun visited Singapore and Malaysia to teach the Dharma. He met with the Prime Minister of Malaysia, Dr. Mahathir Mohamad.

**September:** The Fo Guang Shan Buddhist Choir performed in Tokyo and Osaka.

**October:** The World Fellowship of Buddhists held its 20th meeting at Nan Tian Temple in Australia. There were representatives from over 80 countries in attendance.

**November:** Fo Guang Shan's Buddhist College, and Songgwang Temple from Korea met to establish and strengthen relations.

**Exercises:**

1. List events showing exchanges between religious leaders.
2. List events receiving honors and awards.
3. List some creative events of Fo Guang Shan.
4. List the educational programs of Fo Guang Shan.
5. List the cultural work of Fo Guang Shan.
6. List the charity work of Fo Guang Shan.

# Glossary

**asuras:** Demigods.

**anagami:** A person who may be born in either the material world or non-material world or spiritual but will never be reborn in the World of Desire (our world).

**Anuttara-samyak-sambodhi** (Sanskrit: "unexcelled complete enlightenment"): Complete, unexcelled enlightenment, an attribute of all Buddhas.

**Arhat:** One who has attained the highest level of Buddhist learning and chooses not to return to the Human Realm.

**Avalokiteshvara:** One of the great Bodhisattvas of Mahayana Buddhism. Avalokiteshvara can manifest in any conceivable form to bring help wherever it is needed.

**bhiksu:** A Buddhist monk.

**bhiksuni:** A Buddhist nun.

**board:** A piece of wood that is used as a sound signal in the monastery.

**Bodhi:** Awakened to one's own Buddha Nature.

**Bodhisattva Precepts:** The fundamental vow of a bodhisattva to save all sentient beings from delusion and suffering.

**Bodhisattvas:** (1) Any person who is seeking Buddhahood. (2) A "realized being" who stands on the edge of nirvana, but remains in this world to help others in achieving enlightenment.

**Qing Qing Shi:** Chinese "清淨士." This is the first stage for monastics in Fo Guang Shan's personnel order. There are six grades for this stage, with each grade lasting for one year.

**Dharma** (Sanskrit: "carrying, holding"): The teachings of the Buddha, which carry or hold the truth.

**Dharmakaya:** The Buddha Nature which is identical with transcendental reality. The unity of the three Buddha bodies. The other two are the Sambhogakaya and the Nirmanakaya.

**Eight Precepts:** For lay followers to experience the monastic way of life, the Buddha set up the Eight Precepts, which the followers observe within one day and one night.

**Eight Supernatural Beings:** Heavenly Realm Beings (Devas), Dragon Gods (Nagas), Night Demons (Yakshas), Gandharvas, Asuras, Garudas, Kimnaras, and Mahoragas.

**Eka-jati-prati-buddha:** One who will become the Buddha in his next life.

**Five aggregates:** The aggregates, which make up a human being. They are: form, feeling, perception, mental formation, and consciousness.

**Five Precepts:** The five basic precepts of Buddhism: no killing, no stealing, no lying, no sexual misconduct, no use of drugs and alcohol.

**Five Vehicles:** 1) The human, 2) the Heavenly, 3) the Shravakan, 4) the Pratyekan Buddha, 5) the Bodhisattvan.

**Fo Guang Shan:** *(Chinese, literally - 'Buddha's Light Mountain')* The largest Buddhist order and temple system in Taiwan. Founded in 1967 by Master Hsing Yun. Fo Guang Shan's main temple and monastery is about thirty-five miles from Kaohsiung.

**Four assemblies:** Upasaka, Upasika, monks, and nuns.

**Four castes:** Religious figures, warriors, merchants, and slaves.

**Four Diamond Dharma Protectors:** in the East—Dhrtarastra, in the South—Virudhaka, in the West—Virupaksa, and in the North—Vaisravana.

**Four elements:** Earth, water, fire, and wind.

**Four great Bodhisattvas:** Avalokitesvara Bodhisattva, Manjusri Bodhisattva, Ksitigarbha Bodhisattva, Samantabhadra Bodhisattva.

**Four Guiding Principles:** (1) giving others what they need in order to lead them to the truth, (2) using affectionate speech for the same reason, (3) helping others for the same reason, (4) adapting oneself to others for the same reason.

**Xiu Shi:** Chinese "修士." This is the third stage for monastics in

Fo Guang Shan's personnel order. There are three grades for this stage, with each grade lasting from three to six years.

**Xue Shi**: Chinese "學士." This is the second stage for monastics in Fo Guang Shan's personnel order. There are six grades for this stage, with each grade lasting from two to three years.

**Human Vehicle**: Having the five precepts as a guiding principle for one's life.

**Qiao Shi**: Chinese "教士." Jiao Shi are male followers who live in the monastery and commit to contributing their whole life to Buddhism. They do not have their hair shaved.

**Kai Shi**: Chinese "開士." This is the fourth stage for monastics in Fo Guang Shan's personnel order. There are three grades for this stage, with each grade lasting from five to ten years.

**Kalpas**: An extremely long period of time.

**Ksitigarbha**: One of the great Bodhisattvas of Mahayana Buddhism. Ksitigarbha Bodhisattva has vowed to remain in the Hell realm until all sentient beings have been released from it.

**Mahayana**: One of the two great branches of Buddhism (Theravada being the other). Mahayana Buddhism stresses compassion above asceticism.

**Maitreya Bodhisattva**: Maitreya is the Buddha of the future. He will be the fifth, and last, earthly Buddha.

**Manjusri**: The Bodhisattva of wisdom.

**Medicine Buddha's Pure Land**: The Medicine Buddha is the Buddha of healing. He presides over the Eastern Pure Land.

**Monastic Precepts**: The precepts for monks and nuns.

**Noble Eightfold Path**: The path leading to enlightenment as taught by Shakyamuni Buddha. It includes: right view, right thought, right speech, right action, right livelihood, right effort, right mindfulness, and right concentration.

**Parinirvana**: The Great Nirvana of the Buddha Shakyamuni.

**Pratyeka Buddha** (Sanskrit: "solitary awakened one"): One who attains enlightenment on his own, without having heard the teachings of a Buddha.

**saha:** This world of delusion, the world in which Shakyamuni Buddha taught.

**Sakrdagami:** Abider in the fruit of a once-returner.

**Samadhi:** A very high level of meditative concentration.

**Samantabhadra:** One of the great Bodhisattvas of Mahayana Buddhism, and one of the four most revered Bodhisattvas in Chinese tradition.

**Sangha:** The Buddhist community. All followers of Buddhism. In Chinese, Sangha usually refers only to Buddhist monks and nuns.

**Seven Sacred Graces:** Faith, upholding the precepts, humility, regret, listening to the Dharma, renunciation and wisdom.

**Seven treasures of the chiliocosm:** gold, silver, lapis lazuli, crystal, agate, rubies, and cornelian.

**Seven Ways to Resolve Disputes:**

1. Each party will voice their views once and respect the decision made by their superior.

2. If someone has a complaint, we should answer truthfully whether the complaint is true or false. We should be responsible to both our own conscience and the Triple Gem.

3. When confronted with mental instability, calm down and repent before the Buddha.

4. If one has erred, one should voice remorse and repent in the presence of a member of the Sangha or before the Buddha.

5. Members who do not admit their wrongdoing will be barred from membership privileges.

6. Disputes should be settled by a five or seven person panel.

7. If both parties can understand and accept responsibility for their mistakes, everything will be resolved.

**Shastras:** Philosophical and didactic commentaries written on Buddhist sutras by Mahayana thinkers.

**Shigu:** Chinese "師姑." Shi Gu are female followers who live in the monastery and commit to contributing their whole life to Buddhism. They do not have their hair shaved.

**Shi:** Chinese "釋" which is the abbreviation of Shakyamuni.

**Shramanera:** Novice monks who take the ten precepts.

**Shramanerika:** Novice nuns who take the ten precepts.

**Shravaka** (Sanskrit: "one who heard"): Originally a reference to the personal disciples of the Buddha. In Mahayana, it means those students who, in contrast to pratyeka buddhas and bodhisattvas, seek personal enlightenment, and can attain this only by listening to the teachings and gaining insight into the Four Noble Truths and the "emptiness" of all phenomena.

**Six Harmonies:** Harmony of precepts, harmony of view, harmony of benefit, harmony of association, harmony of speech, and harmony of mind.

**Six Paramitas:** (Six Perfections) The six "perfections" or virtues practiced by enlightened beings: generosity, upholding the precepts, patience, diligence, meditation, and wisdom.

**Srota apanna:** Stream-enterer. The first of the four stages toward the realization of liberation leading to Arhatship.

**Sudhana-sresthi-daraka:** a young man appearing in the Avatamsaka Sutra who was very open-minded and diligent in learning from different teachers.

**Sutra:** That which is "threaded together," by extension, the sacred writings of Buddhism.

**Da Shi:** Chinese "大師." This is the highest stage for monastics in Fo Guang Shan's personnel order.

**Tathagata:** One of the ten titles of the Buddha.

**Ten directions:** East, west, south, north, southeast, southwest, northeast, northwest, above, and below.

**Ten Evils:** Killing, stealing, sexual misconduct, lying, duplicity, using harsh words, flattery, greed, anger, and ignorance.

**Ten Paramitas:** Generosity, upholding the precepts, patience, diligence, meditation, wisdom, skillful means (upaya), aspiration, the ten powers, and primordial wisdom.

**Ten Wholesome Deeds:** No killing, stealing, sexual misconduct, lying, duplicity, harsh words, flattery, greed, anger, or ignorance.

**Theravada:** One of the two great branches of Buddhism. Theravada Buddhism stresses individual enlightenment above all else.

**Three Dharma Seals:** The three basic characteristics of existence.are impermanence, the interconnectedness of all things (thus the absence of a self or essence of anything), and nirvana.

**Three Learnings:** Precepts, meditation, and wisdom.

**Three Poisons:** Greed, hatred, and ignorance.

**Three Refuges**: Taking refuge in the Buddha, the Dharma and the Sangha.

**Tripitaka:** The canon of Buddhist scriptures.

**Triple Gem**: The Buddha, the Dharma, and the Sangha (the Buddha, his teaching, and the community of Buddhists).

**Tushita Heaven:** The land of all Buddhas who must take one more birth in the human realm. The land of Maitreya Bodhisattva.

**Upasaka:** Lay male Buddhist follower.

**Upasika:** Lay female Buddhist follower.

**Upaya** (Sanskrit: "skillful means"): the methods and skills used by a buddha or bodhisattva to guide others toward enlightenment.

**Vihara:** *(Sanskrit - "sojourning place")* Residences for monks or nuns.

**Vinaya:** Rules of discipline for monastics.

**vipassana:** Contemplation.

**Western Pure Land:** Amitabha Buddha's Pure Land which is located hundreds of thousands of millions of Buddha-lands to the west of our saha world.

**Yu Shan Buddhist music:** Yu Shan is a mountain located in Shan dong Province, Mainland China. During the Wei dynasty (220~264C.E.), the emperor Qiao Zu once visited Yu Shan. He was very impressed by the sounds of chanting in the area. He emulated the melody and made it into Buddhist music.

(c) 2002 Buddha's Light Publishing

by Venerable Master Hsing Yun
translated by Fo Guang Shan International Translation Center
edited by Ven. Miao Jie

Published by Buddha's Light Publishing
3456 S. Glenmark Drive
Hacienda Heights, CA 91745
U.S.A.
Tel: (626) 923-5143
Fax: (626) 923-5145
e-mail: **itc@blia.org**

ISBN: 0-9715612-2-2
Library of Congress Control Number: 2001099613


Cover designed by Mei-Chi Shih